tom
PETERS

ROBERT HELLER

A Dorling Kindersley Book

www.dk.com

Dorling Kindersley

LONDON, NEW YORK, AUCKLAND, DELHI, JOHANNESBURG,
MUNICH, PARIS, SYDNEY and TORONTO

DK www.dk.com

Senior Editor Adèle Hayward
Senior Art Editor Caroline Marklew
Project Art Editor Christine Lacey
DTP Designer Jason Little
Production Controller Elizabeth Cherry

Managing Editor Stephanie Jackson
Managing Art Editor Nigel Duffield

Produced for Dorling Kindersley by
Grant Laing Partnership 48 Brockwell
Park Gardens, London SE24 9BJ
Managing Editor Jane Laing
Project Editor Helen Ridge
Managing Art Editor Steve Wilson

First published in Great Britain in 2000
by Dorling Kindersley Limited,
9 Henrietta Street, London WC2E 8PS

2 4 6 8 10 9 7 5 3 1

Copyright © 2000
Dorling Kindersley Limited, London
Text copyright © 2000 Robert Heller

A CIP catalogue record for this book is
available from the British Library

ISBN 0 7513 0820 X

Reproduced by Colourpath, London
Printed in Hong Kong by Wing King Tong

Author's Acknowledgments
The many sources for this book have been
acknowledged in the text, but I must now
express my great debt to everybody, above
all to the Mastermind himself. Nor would
the book exist but for the inspiration and
effort of the excellent Dorling Kindersley
team – to whom my warm thanks.

Packager's Acknowledgments
Grant Laing Partnership would like to
thank the following for their help and
participation:
Editorial Lee Stacy, Frank Ritter;
Design Sarah Williams;
Index Kay Ollerenshaw.

Publisher's Acknowledgments
Dorling Kindersley would like to thank the
following for their help and participation:
Editorial Josephine Bryan, Claire Ellerton,
Nicola Munro, Jane Simmonds;
Design Austin Barlow, Tracy Hambleton-
Miles, Laura Watson, Nigel Morris;
DTP Rob Campbell, Louise Waller;
Picture research Andy Sansom.

Picture Credits
The publisher would like to thank the
following for their kind permission to
reproduce the following photographs:
Associated Press Ap: 18, Stephan Savola
17, Toby Talbot 89; **Corbis UK Ltd**: Roger
Ressmeyer 4; **Robert Harding Picture
Library**: 41, 101; Image Bank: Steve
McAlister 61, Patti McConville 83; **Frank
Spooner Pictures**: Thierry Buccon-Gibod
96, Liason 65, Wilson 79; **Tony Stone
Images**: G. Brad Lewis 86, Daniel J. Cox
30, Howard Grey 22, Charles Gupton 54,
Pal Hermansen 72, Walter Hodges 37, Ian
Jackson 50, Jon Riley 12, Terry Vine 29;
Times Syndication: 9.

Front jacket: **Times Syndication**.

Contents

The management preacher

Tom Peters built his reputation as the archetype of the evangelical guru on one book, *In Search of Excellence.* Published in 1982, this title has outsold all other management books by millions of copies. Peters and his co-author, Robert Waterman, argued that common observable characteristics were shared by successful large firms, and that chief executives could manage effectively by following strong, simple, top-down policies.

As business became more complex, Peters changed his mind. He has become a spokesman for the left-wing of management thought, the radical critics who call for extreme change. He started by encouraging leaders to leave their offices and "manage by wandering around". He went on to stress that in chaotic times management, too, has to be chaotic, and that small firms are the better models.

Today Peters operates as the arch-revolutionary, the Trotsky of the New Management, urging managers to strive in highly unconventional ways to get the "Wow!" reaction from their delighted customers. His seminars have been described as "Management as Performance Art".

Robert Heller

Biography

Tom Peters has an unusual background for a management guru. Born in 1942, he worked in the Pentagon for two years before studying civil engineering at Cornell. He served in Vietnam, got an MBA at Stanford, and then returned to Washington for a spell at the Office of Management and Budget. He thus brought an unusual breadth of experience and education to McKinsey, the leading management consultancy, which he joined as a consultant in 1974, at a crucial juncture in its history.

At this time, a rival and much younger consultancy, Boston Consulting Group, had seized intellectual leadership in the profession by developing and publicizing its "matrix", which assessed products and businesses by plotting their share of a market against the growth rate in that market. While simplistic, and now long out of favour, the Boston matrix caught the interest of top managers, who saw it as a clear and quick guide to strategic decisions on the best way to invest corporate funds. McKinsey needed a rival product that would steal back its thunder.

The "excellent company" project

In 1977, Peters was assigned to what became known as the "excellent company" project; his brief, to discover what characteristics distinguished the company that excelled in performance from any other firm. The project was joined by two other McKinsey consultants, one of them Robert Waterman, and by two academics: Anthony Athos, an expert on corporate cultures, and Richard Pascale, a student of American and Japanese companies.

The first result of the research was the "Seven-S" formula for analyzing a company (see p. 14). Although "Seven-S" never matched the Boston matrix for popular appeal, Waterman, in talking to one chief executive, was struck by the idea that managing excellent companies produced identifiable, transferrable common practices. Could the essence of excellence be distilled and then instilled into other managements? Using the "Seven-S" formula, he and Peters began their analysis of 43 large US companies whose financial records indicated excellence.

The discovery of eight common characteristics, or attributes, attracted publishing interest, and Peters and Waterman set to work on what proved a highly taxing project for both men – and for their firm, which provided a small army of helpers. Neither had written a book before. Working from home, Peters produced enormous numbers of words, which had to be heavily edited into shape. Nobody had any idea that the result would be much of a success when it was published as *In Search of Excellence* in 1982.

The launch of a writing career

Sales started to advance into the millions as company after company bought the book in volume to give to their executives. The success generated great sums in royalties. Under the consultancy's contracts, any such income belonged not to individual consultants but to the firm. Luckily for him, Peters had left the consultancy a year before publication so was entitled to receive his share of the royalties personally. These royalties and the fame resulting from the enormous success of the book helped him to build an independent and richly successful career as author, consultant (with his own organization, the Tom Peters

Group), and, above all, crusader for his revolutionary, vehement management ideas.

These ideas are not the same ones as those that *In Search of Excellence* promulgated so successfully. In many respects, Peters performed a U-turn after leaving McKinsey and ending his collaboration with Waterman. The latter, altogether a less driven man, stayed on as a McKinsey partner until 1986 and also for some time kept the faith with the large companies, led by IBM, which were the role-models for *In Search of Excellence*. This was despite the evidence – which started to appear soon after publication – that many of the selected companies were deeply flawed.

Over time, three-quarters of the companies featured in the book failed either relatively or absolutely (some very soon). But long before the final failure, Peters was already well launched on his new career as writer, highly paid and much sought-after speaker, and peripatetic consultant. He declared in 1987 that there were no excellent companies; his heroes now were not large businesses, but small ones. He became the Savonarola of management counter-culture – a fiery, theatrical, fiercely critical, inspirational preacher who exhorts his audiences to forget what they (and he) were taught at business school and embrace "revolution".

An evangelical approach

Peters' huge display of nervous energy as he marches round his audience is not assumed. He drives himself ferociously, sometimes over the brink of exhaustion. He has complete command of his material and his audience, developed by years of practice. His skills as a speaker were one reason why *In Search of Excellence* achieved its astonishing breakthrough. He is said to have given "excellence" seminars to 100,000–200,000 people in the three years after publication, and he must have reached far larger numbers through TV appearances. By his marketing efforts, Peters brought the management book down the corporate hierarchy to the ranks of aspiring managers.

The evangelical approach had begun to appear when Peters was still preaching the big company message. He started the "Skunk Camp" in 1984, an annual event the name of which was drawn from "skunkworks", meaning an innovative group established well away from the main corporation (see p. 41). Peters described the delegates as: "Forty brave souls who have been going their own way [and] met in California and swapped tales about the battles fought, the scars accumulated, and the personal and soul-satisfying experiences that have come from watching their people become winners."

Liberating managers

By 1992, when Liberation Management *was published, Peters was urging companies to abandon hierarchy and adopt flexible, free-flowing structures with large, efficient networks.*

In praise of leadership

Peters was moving away from the boardroom and on to his new battleground, in which "skunks" lower down the management structure rebelled against the corporate norms in order to care for customers, innovate, and manage people by exerting individual leadership. The key element here is MBWA: "Management by Wandering Around". With a new co-author, Nancy Austin, Peters published *A Passion for Excellence* in 1989. The subtitle was "The Leadership Difference", and the admired leaders were no longer just corporate chieftains of companies such as IBM, but also people like Frank Perdue of Perdue Farms. The essence of Peters' new enthusiasms was entrepreneurialism.

He has also practised what he preached. The Tom Peters Group, located in Palo Alto in Silicon Valley, is a very active training organization, offering a variety of courses. They range from the Leadership Challenge Workshop ("how to get extraordinary things done in organizations") via Corporate Cultures ("aligning action with values throughout the organization") to Customer Service ("providing distinctive service that Wows the customer"). Peters has nine associates in the firm, which also offers "skilful facilitation" and "strategic consulting". He and his wife, Kate Abbe, whom he describes as "spouse, poet, publisher, pal", live in Palo Alto when not on their farm in Vermont.

The TPG is obviously Tom Peters writ large. As a one-man industry he has reeled off not only books but audio and video programmes galore. There are 20 videos extant, starting with *Excellence: the Film*, which came out in 1985. Although he has so decisively rejected the large companies that were the original models of excellence, Peters is well aware of the continuing brand value of his first book: witness a 1999 audio project, with accompanying paperback, entitled *Excellence Aerobics*. However, the book that launched Peters' career was a suit-and-tie affair; his later work is jeans and open-neck shirt.

Revolutionary message

The flavour of his later work is well communicated by the video title, *Ten Rules for Giving Incredible Speeches and Why They're Irrelevant*, which came out in 1990. He loves to shock and startle with paradox and slangy prose. The editing that pared down *In Search of Excellence* was nowhere visible in *Thriving on Chaos*, published in 1987, which runs to over 500 pages and contains no less than 45 main precepts for managers to follow. It set out the agenda for Peters' future career and for the revolutionary course on which he wished to launch American companies.

From his own point of view, *Thriving on Chaos* and its later variations have worked excellently, even though he has become more and more extreme in presentation and language. In the Nineties *The Pursuit of Wow!* (1994) was "every person's guide to topsy-turvy times", while *The Tom Peters Seminar* (1994) announced that "crazy times call for crazy organizations". It has been said that Peters was lucky in his timing: *In Search of Excellence* brought reassurance to US managements feeling threatened by Japanese incursions; *Thriving on Chaos* offered a new faith to replace the certainties demolished by the 1987 stock market crash.

But the Peters phenomenon is more than good timing. While his work is fallible, and open to critical attack on all sides, he has pounded home the truths derived from the new wave of entrepreneurs. They have shown that what Peters teaches is true: that there is a different, better, and perhaps essential way in which to manage.

1

The discovery of excellence

Imitating the eight key attributes that lead to excellent financial performance **● How the 43 "excellent" companies failed to live up to their billing ●** The appearance of listening to customers as key management practice **● Getting out of the office and walking the plant floors ●** Challenging the corporate world to adopt better ways of managing **● Getting improvements in productivity by going beyond incentive payments ●** Rejecting the model of rational, highly organized, "scientific" management

The purpose of Peters and Waterman's *In Search of Excellence* – to restore intellectual pre-eminence to McKinsey among its corporate clientele – was amply achieved, even though academic and other critics found no difficulty in demolishing the book. In fact, the technique used by Peters and Waterman, basing conclusions on studies of actual corporations, was, and still is, the backbone of academic "research" into management.

The first result of McKinsey's research, the "Seven-S" formula, was as respectable as any academic treatise, although it had been carefully plotted to appeal to a lay audience through its catchily alliterative title. Its seven categories – structure, strategy, systems, style of management, skills, staff, and shared values – provided a reasonably comprehensive guide to analyzing the culture and behaviour of corporations, using non-financial criteria. However, the selection of corporate subjects for the "excellence study", which was started in 1977, was based on financial performance and on the clear implication that imitating those subjects would, in turn, produce a similar performance by the imitators.

The 43 companies chosen for the study, which included such big names as IBM, Johnson & Johnson, Exxon, Procter & Gamble, and General Electric, had for two decades led other businesses in *Fortune* magazine's list of America's 500 largest corporations on six factors:

- Growth in assets
- Growth in equity value
- Ratio of market value to book value
- Return on capital
- Return on equity
- Return on sales

The eight attributes of success

In developing the excellence concept, Peters and Waterman identified eight attributes that they deemed were shared by the selected 43 companies. As with the Seven-S formula, these attributes were all non-financial:

- Bias towards action
- Simple form, lean staff
- Continued contact with customers
- Productivity improvement via people
- Operational autonomy to encourage entrepreneurs
- Stress on one key business value
- Emphasis on doing what they know best ("sticking to the knitting")
- Loose-tight controls

There is an obvious difficulty in proving the existence of these attributes (and in explaining what is meant by "loose-tight"). It may be possible to show that 43 financially successful companies, with high returns on capital, equity, and sales, do indeed share a common characteristic, such as a "bias towards action". But that does not establish any connection between the bias and the return. You can conclude more justifiably from studying Olympic gold medallists in the 100 metres that being black is a common feature. But that doesn't establish African ancestry as a necessary condition, or even an explanation.

"Our fixation with financial measures leads us to downplay or ignore less tangible non-financial measures."
Thriving on Chaos

Unlike the criteria for selecting the 43, none of the eight has the one essential quality for solid comparisons: measurability. How can you calibrate "stress on one key business value" or prove that Company A emphasizes doing what they know best more than Company B? Equally, how can you demonstrate that this difference (which you cannot measure) has any impact (which you also cannot measure) on Company A's superiority of any kind – let alone its financial characteristics? You can measure productivity improvement, true, but how do you separate the improvement achieved by investment, or by higher sales volume, from that supplied by better people management?

Anecdotal evidence

The "evidence" supplied in support of the thesis was mainly anecdotal. The conclusions were only as good as the anecdotes, and, as evidence of corporate excellence, the stories were not very good. They were examples of fine management, possibly, but were they isolated examples, rather than proofs of some general excellence?

If Peters and Waterman had any doubts on this score, they were swept aside in the tide of anecdotal reporting. This is one of Peters' great strengths. He writes and talks vividly about companies and their managers, and the anecdotes in *In Search of Excellence* bear his stamp. For example, Digital Equipment, the computer manufacturer, would have bands of only five to 25 people testing out ideas on a customer, often using cheap prototypes. That took just a few weeks, while the typical company might have had 250 people working on a new product in isolation for 15 months. However, no conclusions could safely be drawn from Digital; it was dominated by one eccentric entrepreneur,

Ken Olsen, who bent the company to his will in often painful manner. His greatest mistake – to disparage and ignore the personal computer – spelt Digital's doom. It became one of the celebrated failures among *Excellence*'s heroes.

In fact, *Excellence* did point out one drawback of the methods employed by Olsen: "At Digital the chaos is so rampant that, one executive noted, damn few people know

Digital's downfall
Ken Olsen founded Digital Equipment in 1957. His eccentric style of management created huge success, but ultimately led to the company's decline. In 1998, it was bought by Compaq Computer.

Mine's a Big Mac
McDonald's, which started life in 1948 as a hamburger stand in San Bernardino, California, was one of the 43 "excellent" companies that has maintained its performance and reputation for years.

who they work for." This chaos, however, was presented by Peters and Waterman as a saving grace, part of the eighth attribute: "loose-tight controls". The looseness, on this reading, was offset by tightness, by the alleged fact that "Digital's fetish for reliability is more rigidly adhered to than any outsider could imagine". The authors were themselves outsiders, of course. But as usual in all anecdotal business studies of this kind, their theory about Digital was not derived from observation from the outside. The observations were selected to support the theory. If you have selected 43 companies as examples of "excellence", you are not looking for evidence of their fallibility. Had they investigated more closely, they would have found their chosen companies lacking, not just on the eight non-financial attributes, but on the very financial criteria that had led to their selection.

From the 43, the authors picked 14 companies as particular examples: Bechtel, Boeing, Caterpillar Tractor, Dana, Delta Airlines, Digital Equipment, Emerson Electric, Fluor, Hewlett-Packard, IBM, Johnson & Johnson, McDonald's, Procter & Gamble, and 3M. Taking ten of these companies, their average position out of *Fortune*'s top 500 companies, over the decade 1971–81, was 243rd for total return to investors and 167th for growth in earnings per share. The 1981 figures for net return on shareholders' equity and net return on sales, while not wonderful, were better (especially the sales number). But long-term performance, rather than that of a single year, was supposed to be the distinction of the chosen few. With the criteria and the conclusions both dubious, *Excellence* was on flimsy ground.

Themes of excellence

For all that, the study laid several foundations for Peters' later thought, even though the ideas he went on to develop seemed so far from those advocated in *Excellence*. It was here that the theme of customer service first surfaced. The authors approvingly quote an IBM marketing supremo (and adulator), Frank (Buck) Rogers: "It's a shame that, in so many companies, whenever you get good service, it's an exception. At such companies, managers know that the best product ideas can come from customers – if you listen intently and regularly." Did it matter that IBM actually failed to practise what Rogers preached? Those virtues *should* have existed, after all.

It was a short step from describing virtue to prescribing it, to laying down (as Peters did in the post-*Excellence* years) the "right" ways to run companies. One of those ways, marking another Peters theme, also surfaced at this early point: MBWA "Management by Wandering Around" (see pp. 37–8). The authors praised bosses who were known for walking the plant floors, men such as Ray Kroc, the chairman of McDonald's, who rightly and regularly visited outlets and assessed them on the factors he held dear: QSC&V (Quality, Service, Cleanliness, and Value).

Innovation is another theme running through all Peters' work. He and Waterman were impressed (as were many others) by 3M, which won fulsome appreciation for being "so intent on innovation that its essential atmosphere seems not like that of a large corporation, but rather a loose network of laboratories and cubbyholes populated by feverish inventors and dauntless entrepreneurs who let their imaginations fly in all directions". The description reads like the unreal nonsense it was. There was greater

"A lot of companies are spending jillions on innovation but all they're producing is the 64th variety of spaghetti sauce. I don't think you get innovation for free. But a lot of it has to do with the spirit of the enterprise."
The Pursuit of Wow!

apparent sense in the fourth Peters theme: that the way to learn better management is to study what other managers actually do and adapt or adopt their methods.

An imaginary reality

The eight attributes were valuable qualities for businesses to have, and far superior to the prevailing norms. Peters and Waterman were, after all, writing for a corporate world that was biased towards inaction rather than action. Far from having simple structures, corporations had convoluted bureaucracies, stuffed with too many staff. They were production-led, inbred, and paid too little attention to what customers wanted in terms of product or service. Their productivity lagged largely because they treated front-line people as mindless cannon-fodder. Any stirrings of entrepreneurship or initiative were stifled by a culture of interference and lack of autonomy. The values and strategy were unclear and cluttered by contradictions.

Far from "sticking to the knitting", that is, staying with what they knew best, typical large companies diversified into areas they knew nothing of. Far from coupling "loose" management with tight controls over finance and reporting, they turned control systems into straitjackets that imprisoned every manager. That was the truth. But *Excellence* succeeded because it blazoned forth an imaginary reality, a non-existent world in which virtue – American virtue – was triumphant:

"The findings from the excellent companies amount to an upbeat message. There is good news from America. Good management practice today is not resident only in Japan. But, more important, the good news comes from treating people decently and asking them to

Knowledge workers
Technology has given people the freedom to work away from their desks, encouraging innovation and creativity. According to Peters, the suited, office-bound executive has become outmoded.

shine, and from producing things that work. Scale efficiencies give way to small units with turned-on people. Precisely planned R&D efforts aimed at big-bang projects are replaced by armies of dedicated champions. A numbing focus on cost gives way to an enhancing focus on quality. Hierarchy and three-piece suits give way to first names, shirtsleeves, hoop-la, and project-based flexibility. Working according to fat rule books is replaced by everyone's contributing."

This was the stuff of dreams. But it conveyed enormous reassurance to the American chief executive. Not only was he now convinced that his company was doing a good job – rather, an excellent one – but it was all his own work. All of the eight attributes were his to command. He could give operational autonomy, ordain contact with customers, "stick to the knitting" by rejecting diversification and concentrating on the company's real strengths, promulgate the core values he had chosen, and so on. As for Japanese competition (barely mentioned in the book), that was irrelevant. Not only could America win: its major companies really were winning, even if the facts of Japanese market penetration showed otherwise.

Faltering giants

The publication of *Excellence* was timely in that it appeared when American business was anxious for comfort. But that was also the point when the mighty were about to fall. Hence, the infamous record of decline and disappointment of the companies featured in the book. The awful setbacks that lay in store for Caterpillar Tractor, Boeing, Digital Equipment, Fluor, McDonald's, and IBM (the star of the book) were general as well as specific. As the US economy faltered, so did its giants. Which came first, the chicken or the egg, was actually irrelevant. It is very likely that any random selection of big US companies would have fared as badly as the heroes of *Excellence*.

Peters and Waterman's thesis about US excellence may have contributed to the complacency. But behind the cheerleading for American management lay a serious examination of profound changes that truly were being forced on all major companies. The old strategy taught managements to eliminate overlaps, duplication, and waste by concentrating on massive production runs. Provided that everything was carefully and formally co-ordinated, big would always be better. Scale economies took companies a massive stride towards being the low-cost producer, and thus the surefire winner.

What mattered most to customers in this old business model was cost. The authors argued, however, that economies of scale were losing their sovereign power, diminishing in value as customers sought variety, and as quality (or value for money) became decisive. They were right. Quality, moreover, was no longer just a matter of inspection, discipline, control, and exhortation. As taught by the new quality gurus (almost all of them Americans, as it happened) and actually practised by the Japanese, quality was a new way of corporate life.

This style of corporate life sprang from the intelligent management of people and from obtaining their collaboration in the work of continuous improvement. The authors turned their back on the traditional idea that if you got the incentives right, productivity would inevitably follow, and that income was all. In this theory, the right payment schemes, giving top rewards to top performers, and weeding out the 30 to 40 per cent of deadwood (that is,

"It doesn't matter whether... you are section head or chairman of the board. If you knowingly ignore a tiny act of lousy service or poor quality, you have destroyed your credibility and any possibility of moral leadership on this issue." *Thriving on Chaos*

those who did not want to work anyway), would encourage people to do things right and work intelligently. Here, too, the conventional ideas were being displaced as the knowledge workers moved to the fore; that is, professionals who "identify themselves by their own knowledge rather than by the organizations that pay them" (Drucker – *Management Challenges for the 21st Century*, 1999).

Rejecting rational management

The changes under way in the business world were incompatible with the traditional view of the corporation as a machine. Peters and Waterman rejected the idea that analysis was all, and that "scientific", rational management was always the answer. This rational approach held that good market research helped to avoid big foolish decisions, and that financial analysis could be usefully applied to risky investments such as research and development. In addition, budgeting was an obvious model for long-range planning, and forecasts were plainly important. It seemed only sensible to set hard numerical targets on the basis of those forecasts.

The rationalists saw the top manager's job as making decisions, getting them right, balancing the corporate portfolio of investments, and buying into the attractive industries. He used his subordinates as controllers whose job was to keep things tidy and avoid surprises; they worked within a detailed organizational structure, wrote clear job descriptions, ensured that every possible contingency was accounted for, issued orders, resolved issues in black and white terms, and regarded people as factors of production. Effective planning went hand-in-hand with a massive commitment of resources to the chosen projects.

In Search of Excellence rejected this model, even though Peters and Waterman, as management consultants, belonged to a breed of professionals whose bread-and-butter (and plenty of honey) derived from applying the rational approach indiscriminately to all their clients. But the authors' critical attitude was straight commonsense. Economies are not the only things that matter in business, and, what's more, all really good companies have excellent policies that analysis would certainly rule out as uneconomic. The pair cited the over-commitment to reliability by Caterpillar Tractor ("48 hours parts service anywhere in the world, or CAT pays").

Allowing for mistakes

Peters thus began his conversion to "crazy" management by underlining the problems of being too rigidly rational, arguing that rigidity rules out experimentation and does not allow for mistakes. The authors pointed out that the IBM 360 was a vast success of American business history, yet its development was sloppy. IBM's response was to design a product-development system that would prevent such a problem recurring. However, as IBM chairman Frank Cary said, "Unfortunately, it will also ensure that we don't ever invent another product like the 360." The system was duly scrapped, to Peters' approval, but IBM never did "invent another product like the 360". It did have a massive big hit with the Personal Computer, true, but that was originally developed outside the IBM system altogether, in a separate organization at Boca Raton, Florida.

This anecdote illustrates the central difficulty on which the *Excellence* thesis foundered. In management, there is an undeniable conflict between the need for control (which is real) and the need for freedom (which is essential for creativity). In *Excellence*, the authors tried to balance these two opposites but did not quite succeed. Waterman, in his later books, continued with this difficult exercise. Peters, on the other hand, lost patience and proceeded to tilt the balance decisively towards freedom.

Ideas into action

- Study what other managers do and adapt or adopt whatever works.

- Tear down cultures of bureaucracy, interference, and lack of autonomy.

- Dedicate "champions" to leading the drive for innovation in products and processes.

- Break the business down into small units with "turned-on people".

- Ensure staff collaborate to achieve continuous improvement in performance.

- Put customer satisfaction ahead of numerical targets and financial goals.

- Avoid rigid management that rules out experiment and trial and error.

Filling a gap in the market

The astonishing success of *In Search of Excellence* in 1982 turned Peters from a management consultant into a superstar, although he shared the limelight and glory with his co-author, Robert Waterman.

The flamboyant drive that Peters brought to everything was a major factor in the mounting millions of sales. On his own account, the sales were no accident, but the result of "an unsystematic (but in retrospect thorough) word-of-mouth campaign" that began two years before publication.

Peters turned the book's long gestation period into an advantage. In 1980, a 125-page presentation of "what became the book's principal findings" was bound and "circulated surreptitiously among business executives". In all, the authors printed 15,000 copies to satisfy what Peters (with a touch of bombast) calls "underground demand". He adds that at least an equal number of photocopies swelled "the network".

The pair also "assiduously courted opinion leaders in the media over several years". According to Peters, this paid off within days of the book's launch. He says that "supportive reviews" appeared, and the network "hurried to buy the real thing, often in bulk for their subordinates". Other, differing accounts record that *Excellence* came out to largely hostile reviews and achieved only modest sales – until suddenly, apparently spurred by one company's large purchases, the book took off.

Effective marketing

Peters claims the book could not have been better marketed than if the whole process had been planned meticulously. But the success owed less to Peters' word-of-mouth campaign than to lucky timing – its publication coincided with mounting anxiety about the US economy – and to the simple appeal of the book's basic idea. This theme was first exposed in a *Business Week* article that summarized the eight attributes of excellence, but more important was the notion that excellence was transferrable by example: study how top performers performed, and you, too, could have a top company.

"When Aunt Mary has to give that nephew of hers a high school graduation present and she gives him *In Search of Excellence*, you know that management has become part of the general culture." Peter Drucker

This has been the foundation of Peters' preaching and practice ever since, and its critics fastened on the simplistic weakness of the approach. The management expert Peter Drucker commented on how easy *Excellence* made management seem: "All you had to do was put the book under your pillow and it will get done." But, of course, that was the book's secret. It not only made a difficult subject seem easy, but promised easy results. All the same, selling five million copies in three years indicated a huge, yawning gap in the market, a demand not so much for the book's content as for its talismanic effect.

That must be true if Peters is right in estimating that over half the purchasers did not even turn the pages of *Excellence*. Half-a-million, he thought, had read five chapters. A mere 100,000 had read the whole book. In other words, the market had been defined, but not yet fully exploited. Making good that defect became the engine of Peters' future career.

2

Managing with passion

How Peters turned against some old heroes and found new ones ● **Abandoning the "vaunted American management mystique" and going "back to basics"** ● The two ways of getting "superior performance over the long haul" ● **Why winners succeed, not through cleverness, but attention to detail** ● Managing by wandering around ● **Why only one perceived reality counts – the customer's view** ● Championing "skunks", the rule-breakers and individualists, to promote innovation

Peters' rejection of the large company models for *Excellence* was eminently justifed by their performance after the book's publication in 1982. The relative or absolute failure of heroes like IBM became a running joke. It led both Peters and Waterman to query and analyze what had gone wrong. Waterman still believed in big companies, especially IBM, long after Peters had turned against the old heroes. But Peters' total conversion was by no means immediate.

For his next book, *A Passion for Excellence*, co-written with Nancy Austin and published in 1985, he still stuck to "old friends", including IBM, Hewlett-Packard, and 3M. He praised a Ford plant, too, and (in contrast to the all-American *Excellence*) found European heroes like Marks & Spencer and the Scandinavian airline, SAS. But brand-new US names also joined the pantheon, some of them plucked from obscurity, like Stew Leonard's, a one-store Connecticut operation selling milk, cheese, rolls, and eggs, or Sunset Scavengers in the San Francisco Bay area ("most say the best-run garbage company in America").

Other newcomers to Peters' admiration, however, were far bigger. They included the manufacturer of Goretex, the "breathing" synthetic fibre, Milliken & Company, the privately owned textile giant, and Domino's Pizza, created by a self-help fanatic named Tom Monaghan. Some of the new heroes were propelled into lasting management fame by Peters' blessing. However, the kiss of death that disfigured *In Search of Excellence* was still present. The airline People Express, which ranked, in some respects, as the fastest-growing business in the history of the US, was heading for a final crash. And then there was Apple Computer, whose "free-form organization and unbridled enthusiasm may well be the company's most lasting contribution to the US business scene". Apple, unlike People Express, survived, but its disorganization and lack of bridles almost killed the PC pioneer.

With such high-profile examples, Peters was still adding to what he called the "vaunted American management mystique", even though "it had quickly turned out to be largely just that – mystique".

Back to basics

Peters concluded that the "battering" taken by American business during the 1981–83 recession (which bridged the publication of *In Search of Excellence*) had "humbled every American manager". There was no trace of humility in *Passion*, however, save for a rhetorical warning: "Is there anyone who thinks the recovery means we're permanently out of the woods?"

But Peters believed that a path led through the trees and to the high upland beyond. For the first time, he preached "revolution". The upheaval involved, though, was far from cataclysmic. He sounded the familiar call of "back to basics". Companies had departed from these basics as they adopted the "management systems, schemes, devices, and structures" promoted during the past quarter of a century:

"The average employee can deliver far more than his or her current job demands and far more than the terms 'employee empowerment', 'participative management', and 'multiple job skills' imply."
The Tom Peters Seminar

"Each such scheme seemed to make sense at the time. Each seemed an appropriate answer to growing complexity. But the result was that the basics got lost in a blur of well-meaning gibberish that took us further and further from excellent performance in any sphere. We got so tied up in our techniques, devices, and programs that we forgot about people − the people who produce the product or service and the people who consume it."

In most companies, there was too great a distance between top management and these two vital groups of people: staff and customers. Peters stressed the importance of labour relations, listening to what the workforce has to say, acting on what one hears, and treating them as full partners (although he rather spoilt his case by naming IBM, which did nothing of the sort, as a star example). He emphasized that going "back to basics" did not mean going back but going forward − even if some companies had, in fact, been practising the basics for decades.

What were these basics? How should companies achieve sustainable growth and equity? Peters could not even find "pride in one's organization and enthusiasm for its works" indexed in 25 leading textbooks on management. Nor could he find much about other key concepts, even leadership, which he felt was "crucial to the revolution now under way − so crucial that we believe the words 'managing' and 'management' should be discarded". In contrast to the images of management − "controlling and arranging and demeaning and reducing" − leadership connoted "unleashing energy, building, freeing, and growing".

Peters was very conscious that this sounded uncomfortably like a change from "tough-mindedness" to "tenderness". Concepts like value, vision, and integrity look "soft" to managers who want to produce "hard" results where it counts and is counted: in balance sheets and on bottom lines. So Peters went far, probably too far, to emphasize that his new heroes, such as Perdue Farms, relentlessly applied "the pressure to perform", and, indeed, that the pressure was "nothing short of brutal". These were "no-excuses" environments "where extraordinary results are... routinely expected because the barriers to them have been cleared away".

Creating a paradox

The subordinates could be forgiven for thinking they had jumped out of the frying pan of management control into the fire of "radical decentralization", from "obey – or else" to "succeed – or else". Peters was aware of the paradox, which he said was epitomized by the businesses that served as his new models. He maintained that, "All are tough as nails and uncompromising about their value systems, but at the same time they care deeply about and respect their people; their very respect leads them to *demand* (in the best sense of the word) that each person be an innovative contributor."

Here Peters fell into two traps. First, he repeated the error of hero-worship exhibited in *In Search of Excellence*: misplaced confidence that "superb" chiefs could be identified and that their principles and behaviour were transferrable. Second, he tried to reconcile the irreconcilable – a hard-driving boss with people who are supposed to drive themselves. The first error would be revealed by events like the total failure of People Express and the slump of IBM into heavy losses. The second error was simply accepted. The paradox could not be avoided:

"We must confront the paradox, own it, live it, celebrate it if we are to make much headway in achieving excellence."

Living a paradox sounds complex, but Peters was adamant about the essential simplicity of his new model. "Many accused *In Search of Excellence* of over-simplifying... we have reached the opposite conclusion. *In Search of Excellence* didn't simplify enough!" He and Austin had reduced the creation and sustaining of "superior performance over the long haul" to "only two ways". They were, first, to "take exceptional care of your customers... via superior service and superior quality", and, second, to "constantly innovate". As the authors wrote, "That's it".

Even Peters realized this was too extreme. Firms also needed sound financial controls and sound planning, which he viewed not as a luxury but as a necessity. And "turned-on people" were essential to success. He recognized, too, that businesses can suffer from external forces, such as an overvalued currency: "but one sustains performance by adding enough value to the product so that it is profitably saleable despite international monetary variability". These were significant corrections to the simple two-way model, but they did not address its main weaknesses.

What did "exceptional care", "superior service", and "superior quality" actually mean? More important, how were they to be obtained? True, innovation was important – but surely not as important as the nature of the innovation? Which products, services, or markets did you choose? Peters resembled a parent who tells children to be good, to which they all naturally agree. But the specifics are crucial. Peters thought that the good lay in the detail. He observed, "The winners stun us not by their cleverness, but by the fact that every tiny aspect of the business is just a touch better than the norm." However, the devil is in the detail, too.

Managing by wandering around

According to Peters, the main managerial productivity problem in America was that managers were remote from the detail – by which he meant that they were out of touch with their people and their customers. Peters' answer to the problem was "the technology of the obvious". The way in which leadership became effective in any well-run organization, be it a school, hospital, bank, single-store operation, or industrial enterprise, was MBWA – "Management by Wandering Around". In *A Passion for Excellence*, Peters gave several examples of MBWA, applied in "bugging [that is, bothering] customers", "naive listening" (that is, with a completely open mind), treating the supplier as a customer, and so on.

Peters reeled off lists of questions, all of them pertinent, such as: "What is the frequency of 'all-hands' meetings? Why? Could you do more?" This hardly adds up to "technology of the obvious" or anything else for that matter. Peters was really urging the case for hyperactive, out-of-the-office, interventionist top management. The

Communicating face to face
Management by Wandering Around – irregular, informal meetings with staff, customers, and suppliers in their places of work – is how, according to Peters, managers become effective leaders.

flavour (he referred to it as the "smell") is clear from the following seven injunctions:

- Publicize the fact that you are out wandering 50 per cent of the time, and that your colleagues are as well (if you and they are).
- Be meticulous in having meetings in others' offices/spaces rather than yours.
- Evaluate managers in part — and directly — on the basis of their people's assessment of how well/how frequently they are in touch.
- Fire a supervisor who doesn't know all his people's first and last names.
- Hold meetings and reviews in the field.
- Start randomly popping into offices and asking the inhabitants why they aren't out.
- If you are a manufacturing, or an R&D boss, etc., make sure you have a second office in the workplace.

The MBWA prescription suffered from the same authoritarian, top-down bias ("Fire a supervisor"...) as the formula put forward in *In Search of Excellence*. And although there was an eighth injunction that suggested that the boss should hold back from bossing, Peters and Austin significantly found this "an especially tough one. When you're harried and need some information badly, and only Mrs X has it, and you discover upon calling that she's out on a field visit — don't call her in the field and tell her to rush back and get the answer. *Wait!*" Nevertheless, the hands-on top management implicit in MBWA was greatly preferable to the desk-bound, out-of-touch alternative, even though the better mode could hardly support a full-length book, and particularly one that ran to more than 400 pages.

Applying integrity

Peters and Austin went on to develop a theory of business that, they claimed, was permeated by MBWA, but which, in reality, was largely independent of that panacea. They were aware of the danger that managers would pay only lip-service to their teachings, and chose to describe this as lack of "integrity". They observed that "virtually every device we suggest is doomed to be useless unless applied with integrity". Despite Peters' insistence on the simplicity of this approach, their ideas added up to an incredibly complex and heavy burden: "Ah yes, that's it. A million devices, each important – *and* integrity."

Starting with the customer, managers were urged to use "common courtesy" as "the ultimate barrier to competitor entry". As for what the customer was sold, Peters said flatly that there was no such thing as a commodity. The job of the manager was to observe the "evidence favouring differentiation and higher-value-added products and service", which was "close to overwhelming". Acting as if cost and price were the only variables that could be manipulated was wrong. Peters agreed that "market dominance combined with lowest industry cost is nice if you can achieve it". However, he stressed that quality should always be the driving force and come first.

Quality, moreover, is in the eye of the beholder, the customer. Peters was one of the first management thinkers to emphasize that "*perception* is all there is…. There is only one perceived reality, the way each of us chooses to perceive a communication, the value of a service, the value of a particular product feature, the quality of a product." Coming to grips with these perceptions is the essence of "managing and marketing. And leading." Quality is not a technique, but a product of managers who "live the quality message with passion, persistence, and, above all, consistency", who judge and measure their success by customer perceptions, and who follow no less than 22 "aspects of a true customers-first orientation". The authors admitted, though, that this was an "idealized portrait", and they knew of no company that managed to follow all 22 precepts with equal intensity.

Encouraging innovation

An "idealized portrait" is a description that can also be applied to the whole of *A Passion for Excellence*: Peters and Austin repeat their disclaimer when listing the ways (23 this time) to know when your company "smells" of innovation. This inability of companies to live up to the innovatory ideal is inevitable, provided you accept the book's portrayal of innovation as essentially contrarian. The great innovators behave illogically. They succeed by ignoring five "popular myths" (see below) and following "counterpoint" approaches.

- Myth One: Substantial strategic or technological planning greatly increases the probability of a "no surprises" outcome.
- Myth Two: Complete technical specifications and a thoroughly researched market plan are invariant first steps to success.
- Myth Three: Time for reflection and thought built into the process are essential to creative results.
- Myth Four: Big teams are necessary to blitz a project rapidly, especially a complex one.
- Myth Five: Customers invariably only tell you about yesterday's needs.

Skunk-free zone
The large, sprawling offices and rigid systems typical of most big businesses do little to encourage innovation. Peters believes that skunkworks are far superior for development of new ideas.

Peters had been impressed in his researches by the "inherent sloppiness" of innovation. Its "given precondition" is a "messy world". The necessary solution had three parts, each one leading on to the next: "experimentation: champions: decentralized bands". The authors gave these stages nicknames: "tries, skunks, and skunkworks". Skunks are the iconoclasts, the rule-breakers, the individualists who strive to accomplish new things and mostly suffer for it, either failing or being fired. They are safer in skunkworks, separate units, preferably set apart from the main company, possibly in rural seclusion, and given a specific, innovatory remit. Management's task is to generate the right climate for experimentation, creativity, and individualism. This climate requires managers to take advantage of that "inherent sloppiness" of innovation – swimming upstream against the myths.

Peters and Austin did not turn these mythical propositions upside down, but their "counterpoints" offered a different mindset. True innovators based their work on uncertainty and ambiguity, experimented, lived by the one dictum "try it now", used small teams, and drew their inspiration from "forward-looking customers", who are "usually years ahead of the rest, and are the best source of leading-edge innovation". The authors ignored the fact that the great innovations of their time, including the mainframe computer, the PC, and the jetliner, were generated internally, often without any customers in sight.

Rejecting bigness

That is also true of many lesser innovations, including the 3M Post-It pads which *A Passion for Excellence* selects as a prize example. The book cites 3M as one of its key sources in learning about the basics of "constant innovation". Yet Peters does not mention the company's almost lethal opposition to the Post-It idea during most of its development. This emphasizes the point that his anecdotes are highly selective. He rejoices in the time he and Austin spent "with today's great entrepreneurs", stars who could do no wrong: or, rather, Peters concentrated on what they appeared to do right. Yet he denied they were the most important people who had shaped his thinking:

> "Most important are those whose names are absent from these pages. Tens of thousands have attended our seminars. They're often enmeshed in stodgy, bureaucratic organizations. Yet they've had the guts to try again, after years of depression and suppression of their ideas. They're out wandering, and proud of it. Out nurturing skunks. Out celebrating their people's successes."

Peters was thus beginning to sing a different tune, asserting that he and Austin were not fans of the executives of the Fortune 500 companies, but "special fans of those, most often in the mid-sized or smaller companies, who are making the American economy grow". In talking to and writing for the dominant companies, Peters had come to believe that he was preaching, not to the converted, but to the unconvertible. It was a short step from that conclusion to his next phase – that of the corporate revolutionary.

Ideas into action

- Be "soft" in managing people, "hard" in expecting good performance.

- Take exceptional care of customers through exceptional quality and service.

- Stay away from your desk as much as you possibly can, and keep in touch with your staff.

- Remember that price and cost are not the only variables in business.

- Live the quality message with "passion, persistence, and, above all, consistency".

- Generate a climate that encourages iconoclasts, rule-breakers, and individualists.

- Ignore the myths of innovation, and rely on forward-looking customers.

Achieving Excellence

om Peters' and Robert Waterman's concept of imitating excellence is one you can try out yourself. Find an excellent role model, either an individual or a company, analyze what makes them successful, and relate their methods to you and your organization's needs.

Imitating excellence

You can learn some valuable lessons in the pursuit of excellence from observing other managers from a distance – so long as you bear the following four principles in mind:

The Four Principles of Excellence
1 Excellent financial results cannot be equated with excellence: results may not last, and may not spring from superior management.
2 Your observations should relate to your needs and circumstances: avoid following courses of action that add no value to your business.
3 Shun lip-service. Methods or approaches that suit you and your business should be sought out, adopted, and adapted.
4 Any remedy is only good for as long as it works: do not become slavishly committed to a modus operandi for ever.

The eight attributes of success

In addition to observing the four principles listed above, use the eight attributes of success described by Peters and Waterman (see p. 15) to provide a valuable checklist and a spur to striving for excellence. These attributes translate into the following highly penetrating personal questions to ask yourself:

- What is the time-lag between your confronting an issue and reaching a decision, and between having made the decision and taking action?
- Do you use the fewest possible people for the highest possible output in the most effective possible set-up?
- Are you in regular, personal contact with customers, and do you use the contact constructively to increase their satisfaction?

TOM PETERS

- Do you manage people policies in order to achieve rising productivity and employee satisfaction?
- Do you delegate fully and effectively, allowing your staff the freedom to do their best?
- Do you have one strong guiding principle?
- Do you concentrate on what you are really good at?
- Do you keep tight control over the "housekeeping", while allowing plenty of latitude in creative work?

You will probably find yourself unable to answer "Yes" to all eight questions. It is extremely unlikely that you, your company, or your unit, are perfect on all eight counts. Go back and look at the questions to which you answered "No", work out what you need to do, then take steps to change the negatives to positives.

Financial indicators

It is significant that none of the eight attributes refers to financial results. This is because the attributes are concerned with your performance as a manager, and financial results are a product of your performance, not the performance itself. All the same, in addition to the eight key attributes, there are five financial questions that will give you vital indicators of how you are performing:

The Five Financial Questions
1 Are you creating wealth?
2 How highly do investors rate your company?
3 How efficiently are you investing capital?
4 How well are you using the shareholders' money?
5 How effectively are you managing costs and revenues and thus the all-important gap between them?

Balance is everything: you can have excellent results on all five counts while managing poorly in key aspects, but you are not managing well if your answers to the five questions are negative. Remember, the proof of excellence is excellent results – financial or non-financial.

1 Confronting problems

Once you have identified any problems in your performance, or in the performance of your unit or organization, set about solving them. Do not be afraid to challenge the status quo.

Reasons for failure

The lessons of failure are invaluable, but only if you learn from them – and act. The way to deal with failures is to ask why they have occurred.

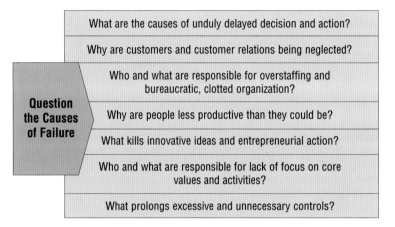

Question the Causes of Failure

What are the causes of unduly delayed decision and action?

Why are customers and customer relations being neglected?

Who and what are responsible for overstaffing and bureaucratic, clotted organization?

Why are people less productive than they could be?

What kills innovative ideas and entrepreneurial action?

Who and what are responsible for lack of focus on core values and activities?

What prolongs excessive and unnecessary controls?

Identifying root causes

Try to identify the root causes of failure. Your instinct will probably be to blame the management. You are part of the management. Delve into the specifics. Some of your explanations may be:

- Too many committees/levels of management.
- Insistence on "the way we do things round here" and therefore resistance to change and reform.
- Rewards/bonuses and staff appraisals do not take customer satisfaction into account.
- Nobody acts on employees' ideas for improving their work.
- A climate of fear penalizes failure and discourages initiative.
- Staff do not share in the shaping of the vision or the plans.
- Rule books and financial controls dominate and therefore hinder management processes.

TOM PETERS

Overcoming failures

You may feel that all the root causes of failure are outside your control. Peters will have none of that – and he is plainly right. If you are not a "skunk", a rule-breaker, innovator, and individualist, why not? You can always learn how to become one.

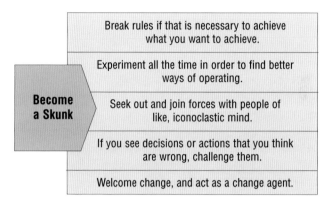

	Break rules if that is necessary to achieve what you want to achieve.
	Experiment all the time in order to find better ways of operating.
Become a Skunk	Seek out and join forces with people of like, iconoclastic mind.
	If you see decisions or actions that you think are wrong, challenge them.
	Welcome change, and act as a change agent.

If you do not strive to become a skunk, then you are not really entitled to complain about your "stodgy bureaucratic organization". If you wait for the people at the top to act, the company (and your job) may be in crisis before anything happens.

Unleashing creativity

The opposite of bureaucracy is innovation, another *Excellence* theme. Accept some disorganization. Try to find assignments in what Peters calls "decentralized bands" in which you can apply freedom rather than control to win success. He is certain that innovators function best when set free (in a separate department, or "skunkworks") to follow anarchic non-rule rules:

- Cherish untidiness, uncertainty, and ambiguity.
- Experiment, experiment, experiment.
- Try it now.
- Appoint champions to head small teams.
- Have "lead customers" with whom you work on innovations hand-in-glove.

Be brave: you have been born in fortunate times. Today skunks are more likely to win – and less likely to be fired.

2 Leading from the front

Peters stresses the importance of leadership, rather than mere management, in the pursuit of excellence. There are four functions in the practice of management that differentiate between leaders and administrators. Strive to fulfil the role of leader.

The Four Differentiating Functions			
1 Controlling others	**2** Organizing work	**3** Facilitating success	**4** Building the business

Leader or administrator?

If you spend most of your time on functions 3 and 4, you are a leader. If 1 and 2 dominate, you are more of an administrator. "Admin" matters a great deal, but leadership is what makes the vital difference to corporate achievement and personal careers.

Balancing needs

One of the leader's key roles is to decide when to sacrifice one good in part for the sake of another. For example, you have to balance the "hard" need to press people to achieve the best results with the "soft" need to encourage self-motivation and individual initiative. Learn to apply pressure in a way that achieves a successful balance.

Leading by example

The impact of an enthusiastic, deeply interested, friendly leader is bound to have a positive effect on others.

- Always show your pride in the company and in your people.
- Be enthusiastic about what you or others are thinking/doing.
- Delegate authority to people and encourage them face-to-face.
- Visit colleagues and customers in their own "space".
- Make impromptu visits, not to check up on people, but to inform yourself about their work and share their enthusiasm.
- When you are in your office, operate an "open-door" policy.
- Hold frequent meetings with everybody present and involved.

Leadership is not a solo activity. Your success as a leader depends on your team's success, and your respect for each other must be mutual.

TOM PETERS

3 Aiming for perfection

Tom Peters and Nancy Austin admitted proudly to simplifying the business of succeeding in business. Their basic principles number only three and need only six words. Live up to those principles – though you will find it is by no means simple.

The Three Principles of Successful Business		
1 Superior quality	**2** Superior service	**3** Constant innovation

Customer care

The aim of excellence is to combine quality, service, and innovation so as to add exceptional value in the eyes of the customer. You are aiming for perfection, though in the knowledge that in "customer care" perfection can rarely be achieved. Use the following eight rules of customer care as a guide to working towards perfection:

- Continually assess levels of service quality by both quantitative and qualitative methods.
- Aim for continuous improvement in the quality of the product and the service.
- Pay close attention to detail, and make sure others do likewise.
- Manage by wandering around your business.
- Manage by wandering around your customers.
- Be incredibly polite and helpful to your customers, and ensure that everybody else in your team is, too.
- Listen to what your customers tell you, and act on it.
- Understand that perception is reality: what the customer thinks is right, even if you think it is wrong.

Placing value before price

The last two rules also apply to innovation – customers are excellent sources of product ideas, and their perceptions will determine whether the innovation succeeds or fails. Peters strongly advises companies to pursue differentiated products and services with higher added value, because value is more important than cost or price. Studies confirm that Peters is right. Customers will happily spend more for higher value. That is the pay-off for true excellence.

3

Practising the theory of chaos

Realizing there are no "excellent" companies ● **Four mega-problems: unpredictability, technological advance, demanding customers, outdated assumptions** ● The five guides for management in "a world turned upside down" ● **"Loving change, tumult, even chaos" as a prerequisite for survival** ● Specializing to create niche markets and differentiate your products and services ● **Ask: "How is the business positioned in the customer's mind?"** ● How to make managers feel involved

By the mid-Eighties, Peters had concluded that nothing in the status quo was defensible, including large companies in general. Irresistible economic, social, and technological forces had changed the world completely and made the model identified in *In Search of Excellence* obsolete. The need was for highly adaptable companies and leaders capable of *Thriving on Chaos*, the title of Peters' next book.

The myth of excellence

In *Thriving on Chaos*, Peters discovered the "upside-down world". He had talked about "revolution" in the previous book, and now he built *Thriving on Chaos* entirely round that concept. This was the "handbook for a management revolution". In *In Search of Excellence*, Peters and Waterman had looked at American industry and pronounced its leaders "excellent". Now Peters, speaking alone, said tersely: "Excellence Isn't". Looking at his very own broken idols, Peters drew a drastic conclusion:

> "There are no excellent companies. The old saw, 'If it ain't broke, don't fix it', needs revision. I propose: 'If it ain't broke, you just haven't looked hard enough.' Fix it anyway. No company is safe. IBM is declared dead in 1979, the best of the best in 1982 [by Peters and Waterman, in fact], and dead again in 1986. People Express [Peters' own selection] is the model 'new look' firm, then flops 24 months later."

Peters did not blame these sad events on any bad judgement of his own. An era of "sustainable excellence" had ended. Nobody had a solid "or even substantial" competitive lead any more. The "champ to chump" cycles were getting shorter. Peters noted that some companies were responding by buying and selling businesses "in the brave hope of staying out in front of the growth industry curve". But *Thriving on Chaos* paraded facts that demonstrated "accelerating American decline" in both manufacturing and services. Merging and demerging had little relevance in that context: Peters' damning verdict was that this buying and selling of businesses was "shuffle for shuffle's sake" and "just part of the madness".

Merger-mad managers were taking an unreal route to solve four mega-problems. First, predictability was a thing of the past. Second, technological advance was changing everything. Third, customers were more demanding, with more fragmented tastes. Fourth, as these forces interacted, old assumptions went "askew". One by one, Peters demolished the pillars of conventional thought, starting with "bigger is better, and biggest is best" and "labour... is to be ever more narrowly specialized, or eliminated if possible". He concluded that big firms had *never* been more innovative than smaller ones, or even more efficient.

The Japanese example

Where *Excellence* and its successor had ignored the Japanese, *Thriving on Chaos* recognized the far faster growth in Japanese productivity and embraced "the Japanese passion whose time has come". By that Peters meant smallness. In a curious passage, he dwells on "folding fans, miniature gardening, the tea ceremony" and argues that a "deep-seated Japanese trait" gave Japan an innate advantage in the age of miniaturized electronic products. There is no mention of superior Japanese management. In discussing superior attitudes to labour, Peters couples "long-standing Japanese traditions" with those of Europe. Both

European and Japanese business cultures, he asserted, were "less dependent on big scale, more dependent on broadly skilled labour" and more "conducive to economic success".

In fact, Japanese industry was (and is) dominated by large-scale firms. But in most respects, the Japanese world-class company did provide an excellent model for Peters' painting of the successful firm of the future, described as:

- Flatter (with fewer layers of organization structure)
- Populated by more autonomous units (with fewer central-staff second-guessers, more local authority to introduce and price products)
- Orientated towards differentiation, producing high value-added goods and services, creating niche markets
- Quality-conscious
- Service-conscious
- More responsive
- Much faster at innovation
- A user of highly trained, flexible people as the principal means of adding value

Looking to Japan
In Thriving on Chaos, *Peters acknowledged the rise of Japan's top firms. But the great bulk of his examples were still Americans, whose practice, however, was being influenced by Japan.*

Animating the workforce

The list of model attributes is an oddly restrained ideal for a "handbook for a management revolution". Any management, however conservative, would find this recipe highly acceptable, in theory, if not in practice. Peters had remained more wedded to the conventional corporate lifestyle than he acknowledged. To him, at this stage, the organizational structure was not the problem, which lay rather in the spirit that animated people within the structure. The ideal spirit was enshrined in no less than 45 precepts, which sought to turn the traditional company upside down to match the inverted environment. These precepts fell into five groups, or general injunctions:

■ Create total customer responsiveness.
■ Pursue fast-paced innovation in all areas of the company.
■ Achieve flexibility by empowering all people connected with the organization.
■ Learn to love change (instead of fighting it) to instil and share an inspiring vision.
■ Control by building simple support systems for a world turned upside down.

At first sight, these divisions seem little different from those that Peters had used in *A Passion for Excellence*: common sense, customers, innovation, "people, people, people", leadership. There were major differences, however. Startlingly, "Management by Wandering Around", the cornerstone and essence of the earlier book (see pp. 37–8), had almost vanished from sight. Peters devoted just two pages to MBWA – and that was only to rebut an influential critic who had nominated MBWA as the "most ridiculous recent management fad". But the critic was right in one respect: "wandering" was an ill-chosen word, with its overtones of aimlessness. Now Peters preached "visible management".

Peters' five injunctions were not radical in the light of current preaching, but only in the light of current practice, with its "inflexible factories, inflexible systems, inflexible front-line people – and, worst of all, inflexible managers". Peters demanded flexibility. He devoted much of the book to "exploring what it means to succeed by loving change". That was crucial: "Today, loving change, tumult, even chaos is a prerequisite for survival, let alone success." Again, however, the trumpet call is not matched by revolutionary concepts in the actual recommendations.

For example, under the heading "Financial Management and Control", Peters wrote about the past and present situation (which he described as "Was/Is"): in this case, that meant "centralized, finance staff as cop". The future need (he called this "Must Become") was defined as "decentralized, most finance people in the field as 'business team' members, high spending authority down the line". In the real world, by 1987, that change in deploying and employing financial staff was not revolutionary, but was becoming standard "best practice".

Some of the "Must Become" imperatives are purely aspirational, even optimistic, and not practical guides with measurable dimensions. Thus, sales and service people are no longer to be viewed by other managers as second-class citizens, dominated by moving the product. They are to become "heroes, relationship managers (with every customer, even in retail), [a] major source of value added, [a] prime source of new product ideas". The creation of sales heroes was one of ten prescriptions under a heading dear to Peters' heart: "creating total customer responsiveness".

Customer strategies

The guiding premise of Peters' customer theories is that mass markets have fragmented and are continuing to fragment. The supplier has no viable alternative but to specialize, to create niche markets, and to differentiate his offering from the competition. That premise leads directly to "five basic value-adding strategies":

- The company has to supply top quality, as perceived by the customer.
- Its service also has to be superior, and to emphasize the "intangibles". The motto here is "little things mean a lot", such as calling customers 30 days after delivery to see if they are happy.
- The company has to achieve extraordinary responsiveness to customers.
- It is necessary to be internationalist because of "the true globalization of the economy", in which opportunities are available to smaller firms as well as large.
- Be unique – how a firm (or a division) is positioned in the customer's mind is the key determinant of "long-term success in a chaotic marketplace".

To realize all five strategies, "capability building blocks" are required, one of which is the conversion of salespeople into the heroes mentioned above. Likewise, manufacturing has to be turned into a marketing weapon. A company obsessed with listening, especially to its customers, can "launch a customer revolution", and become "customer obsessed". Peters asserts:

> "Opportunity now lies, not with perfecting routines, but with taking advantage of instability – that is, creating opportunities from the daily discontinuities of

the turbulent marketplace. To do this, the customer, in spirit and in flesh, must pervade the organization – every system in every department, every procedure, every measure, every meeting, every decision."

"Fast-paced innovation", to which Peters devoted a whole section of *Thriving on Chaos*, is also required for customer responsiveness. He argued that innovation is "a numbers game" – the more avenues you try, the greater the chances of finding one that leads to the pot of gold. So he advocated customer-oriented small starts, rather than "over-emphasizing giant technological leaps". The right methodology is "team-based product development", involving all key functions and key outsiders, such as suppliers, distributors, and customers.

The innovative ideas, too, can come from outside. Peters nicknamed this "creative swiping": you steal and adapt ideas from anywhere, including competitors. In pursuing these ideas, the teams are not to get "bogged down writing long proposals unsupported by hard data". Instead, Peters called for many pilots – "rapid and practical tests in the field". His final piece of advice on the subject was to sell the new product or service by systematic word-of-mouth marketing campaigns. But none of these strategies, he stressed, can be decisive without an innovatory climate brought about by deliberate, pervasive management tactics.

The innovator-in-chief finds and supports "persistent and passionate champions". Without these, he or she cannot hope to sustain innovation "in the face of low odds and corporate rebuffs". Peters called for any "silly" rules that impeded fast action-taking to be defied. Rather, the manager has to run his or her daily affairs to defend and back innovatory efforts. That means supporting "thoughtful failures" and learning from them. If this all sounded "soft", Peters was not being "soft"; he demanded "hard" number targets, properly measured and used purposefully in reward systems.

As the prescriptions in *Thriving on Chaos* unfolded, so did Peters' new vision of a "newly flexible, responsive, and adaptive organization". More and more, he saw the typical organization as the enemy of progress. His theme had become people. Peters asserted that there was no limit to what the average person could achieve if thoroughly involved. To tap people power most effectively, though, "human-scale groupings" were needed, by which he meant teams, and specifically self-managing ones.

Getting involvement

To promote a greater degree of employee involvement in the company, Peters instructed management to introduce, and apply at all times, what he called the "Five Supports":

- Create "an atmosphere marked by constant opportunities (both formal and informal) for everyone to be listened to – and then recognized for their smallest accomplishments".
- Focus recruitment explicitly on desired values and qualities, such as the ability to work in teams.
- Make training and retraining mandatory to constantly upgrade skills.
- Offer incentive pay, based upon contribution and performance, to everyone.
- Offer "some form of employment guarantee [that is, job security] for a major part of the workforce", if people do perform acceptably.

Although this five-part platform was quite extreme (should one really recognize people "for their smallest accomplishments"?), it was not enough. The enemies of progress had to be attacked directly by removing the "Three Inhibitors". This involved managers in:

■ Abolishing complex structures with too many layers and traditional first-line supervision; stopping the use of the middle manager as "cop and guardian of functional fiefdoms"

■ Turning middle managers from bureaucrats into agents of "true autonomy and speed action-taking at the front line"

■ Eliminating "silly bureaucratic procedures and, worse still, demeaning regulations and dispiriting work conditions"

All this – installing the supports and sweeping away the inhibitors – had to be done "all at once", which Peters admitted was "a tall order". But this is true of the whole *Thriving on Chaos* "handbook". The programme is intimidating, even though Peters had constructed the book as helpfully as possible. It is organized clearly into sections, with summaries at all key points, simple charts, innumerable instructive anecdotes, and many checklists and questions – such as these, on delegation:

■ Have you first transmitted the overarching vision with clarity? That is, does the delegate, through demonstrated behaviour, clearly "buy in"?

■ Have you set high standards in the past that make it clear what level of performance you demand?

■ Have you demonstrated in the past, in small ways, that you trust the delegate's judgement?

Teacher-training

Peters believes that training and retraining should be mandatory, and that staff who are encouraged to upgrade their skills are better motivated and, as a result, greater assets for their company.

Impossible demands

The list of checklists relating to delegation goes on for a dozen questions in all. As this tiny, partial glimpse of the whole shows, *Thriving on Chaos* is truly indigestible – a collection of homilies and prescriptions, which, while mostly excellent and consistent, would swamp any manager who sought to live by the book. Peters was making enormous, impossible demands on leaders. How could anybody with a job to do juggle his 45 principal prescriptions, let alone the hundreds of subordinate recipes? He side-stepped this key issue by presenting the management of impossiblity as the central leadership task: "The core paradox... that all leaders at all levels must contend with is fostering (creating) internal stability in order to encourage the pursuit of continual change."

Peters presented no less than 18 paradoxes (and even they were only "a small sample") which, he wrote, turned conventional assumptions upside down. In fact, many of these paradoxes were fast becoming conventions – such as "more competition requires more cooperation", "more productivity comes from having fewer suppliers", "tighter control can be achieved through more decentralization". The real difficulty is that he was still expecting existing organizations and their leaders to adapt to a new order that challenged every principle of their beings.

Yet his formula for the new leadership was commonplace: leaders had to "develop an inspiring vision", "manage by example", and "practise visible management". Teachers of "leadership" had always offered the same prescription. Peters' recipe for empowerment was equally familiar: "Pay attention", "defer to the front line", "delegate", "pursue 'horizontal' management by bashing bureaucracy".

Within the tried and true formulas, however, the radical prescriptions kept mounting up: for instance, the section headed "40 Factors that, Reinforcing One Another, Induce Flexibility". Peters wanted his leaders to become obsessive about change. He demanded that they make "What, exactly, have you changed?" the most common question in the organization, to be asked at least a dozen times a day. Everyone was to be evaluated on "his or her love of change" – another new, heavy, and ill-defined burden.

At times, Peters seemed to realize that he was asking too much. By page 388, the "all at once" demand of page 282 had been sensibly moderated: "While you can't do 'everything at once', no one prescription makes much sense in a vacuum." Yet Peters ultimately never let reality deflect him from his ideals. He saw *Thriving on Chaos* as the "awesome but minimum acceptable agenda". The only solution was to apply enormous energy: "Every managerial act must be seen as an unequivocal support for urgency in pursuit of constant testing, change, and improvement."

Reaching into the book, managers could pull out many valuable plums that would benefit themselves and their companies. But in teaching how to thrive on chaos, Peters had produced a diet that, swallowed whole, could only have created chaos. That, he was soon to conclude, was not his fault, but that of the large corporate consumer.

Ideas into action

- Create "total customer responsiveness" with superior quality, superior service, and fast reaction.

- Create opportunities from "the daily discontinuities of the turbulent marketplace".

- Have many pilot schemes going – rapid and practical field tests.

- Realize that there is no limit to what involved people can achieve.

- Instigate the five supports of involvement, starting with listening and recognition.

- Eliminate silly bureaucratic procedures, demeaning regulations, and dispiriting working conditions.

- Ask people, "What, exactly, have you changed?", several times a day.

Setting up the Skunk Camp

In Search of Excellence created Peters' reputation and launched him as an independent consultant and guru. It also inspired his flowering as the scourge of big business and the proponent of revolutionary organizational reform.

On leaving both McKinsey and Waterman, Peters took another look at his idols of *Excellence*, and concluded they had failed to change in a world that had altered radically, and that radical change required a radical new management model.

His second book, *A Passion for Excellence*, stopped short (though not very short) of this revolutionary creed. But the creed's inspiration, according to Peters, was one of the heroes of the book: Kelly Johnson. Johnson had created and named the first "Skunkworks" at Lockheed – a "modest-sized band" that, over 44 years, had created 41 new military aircraft, including the renowned U-2, together with working prototypes and production models. According to Peters, Johnson delivered advanced and reliable products "in a tenth the expected time at a tenth the expected cost". Johnson, the "corpocracy beater", became the symbol Peters was seeking for *Thriving on Chaos*.

Seminars for activists

Peters decided that his first book had not been imperative enough. Its recommendations were "nice-to-do" in 1979, when the excellence research began. In the late 1980s, the nice-to-dos had become "must-dos". Writing and speaking were not enough, either. Peters launched what he called a "modest effort of my colleagues and myself to focus on applications of the principles for success we had described". This was "spearheaded" by a five-day executive seminar, entitled "Implementing *In Search of Excellence*", unofficially called the "Skunk Camp".

The first session in September 1984 attracted mostly Peters' "heroes", such as the quality-mad chicken tycoon Frank Perdue. But Peters was surprised and inspired at how the attendance developed: "The regular meetings were dominated by (1) people who headed mid-sized companies and (2) action takers, such as plant or division managers, from giant firms."

"To meet the demands of the fast-changing competitive scene, we must simply learn to love change as much as we hated it in the past."
Thriving on Chaos

These people were "activists, not theorists" with a practical question: "What in the heck are we supposed to do?" Faced, too, by overwhelming evidence that "America wasn't cutting it in any industry", Peters moved from descriptive to prescriptive. "So a nice-to-do 'reduce product development cycle time' became hard-edged", with a 75-per cent target and a two-to-three year time-scale. "An innocuous 'reduce the layers' became a sharp 'no more than five layers'… and 'get rid of all first-line supervisors'."

Peters had found his revolutionary cause. To be excellent was no longer enough, "because 'to be' implies stasis". The only excellent firms were those "that are rapidly evolving" in a new direction: companies that got "everyone involved in almost everything", that "trained like the dickens", and introduced "major pay-for-knowledge and profit-distribution plans". The radical formula was completed by urgency. The new breed of excellent firms did it all "NOW".

Working flexibly

Are you and your organization well equipped for rapidly changing and challenging times? "Chaos" is more than likely to prevail in your own workplace. Make flexibility a priority, both in the systems you establish and in your behaviour and that of the people who work for you.

How flexible is your company?

The flexibility of a company depends on its ability to meet seven requirements. Assess the flexibility of your own organization by answering the questions below relating to these seven needs. Answer on a scale from 1 to 5 where number 5 represents "always", 4 "often", 3 "sometimes", 2 "rarely", and 1 "never". Compare your results with the analysis that follows.

- Does the company respond fast and well to the customer?
- Does it innovate in all areas?
- Is the innovation fast-paced?
- Is everybody treated in a flexible, empowering way?
- Do the organization and its staff welcome change?
- Does management communicate and share an inspiring vision?
- Are support systems and controls simple and effective?

Analysis

A maximum score of 35 is very unlikely, while a score below 28 is unacceptable and indicates that there are improvements to be made. Look at the questions for which you scored between 1 and 4, and work towards converting them to a 5.

Size matters

You will probably find, as Peters suggests, that the larger your organization, the less likely it is to meet the seven requirements for flexibility. But small companies are not without fault, either. Mistreating customers, innovating seldom and slowly, disempowering people, resisting change, functioning without any vision of the future, and operating by strict, oppressive, and often ridiculous controls are common to all types of organization.

If your ideal is to work in a flexible environment (as it should be), do not be inflexible yourself. Be open to innovation, commit to change, respond to customer needs, and build on small but firm foundations.

TOM PETERS

1 Setting the agenda

Whatever the size of your organization, set the agenda for yourself as well as others. If you work for an inflexible organization, you will surely be impeded in managing in the way you think best. All the same, go as far as you can along the Peters road.

Start with yourself

You do not need to have a rebellious nature to adopt your own programme. Valuing innovation and adapting to change should be encouraged by sensible seniors, even if only by lip-service. Refuse to work ineffectively, unless you have absolutely no other option.

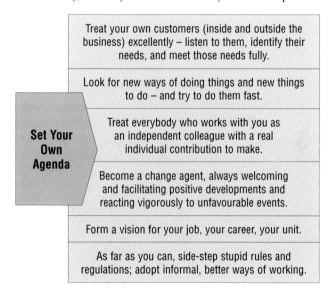

Set Your Own Agenda

Treat your own customers (inside and outside the business) excellently – listen to them, identify their needs, and meet those needs fully.

Look for new ways of doing things and new things to do – and try to do them fast.

Treat everybody who works with you as an independent colleague with a real individual contribution to make.

Become a change agent, always welcoming and facilitating positive developments and reacting vigorously to unfavourable events.

Form a vision for your job, your career, your unit.

As far as you can, side-step stupid rules and regulations; adopt informal, better ways of working.

Broaden your range

A lot depends on your colleagues: seek out those who feel the same way as you do, and make them your allies. If it is within your power, divide your staff into the smallest possible groups consistent with getting the task done efficiently and properly. If one person can see a particular task through from start to finish, then that is the best plan to follow. Such people will belong to a larger grouping, but allow them, too, to set their own agenda.

2 Involving others in change

"Get everyone involved in almost everything," says Peters. Start by listening to your staff. People respond well to being asked for their informed opinions, and you will benefit from their inside knowledge. But you need to do more than just listen. You must act, and doing that will lead to changing accepted polices and practices.

Going beyond limitations

Unfortunately, lip-service is especially common when managers talk about involving or empowering people, and you may well find yourself working "against the organization". Check how many of the following features characterize your company:

- Complex structure
- Too many layers
- Traditional front-line supervision
- Functional separatism
- Bureaucratic procedures
- Demeaning regulations
- Dispiriting work conditions

If any of these apply, ask yourself if you are at all responsible for perpetuating such corporate vices. Ask your staff what improvements they would like to see, and adopt the most useful suggestions. This not only raises morale but may also save expenditure.

Involving people is a two-way process. The following questions will enable you to focus on achieving objectives and to mobilize other, truly involved people to do the same. If your answers are not all "Yes", change your ways. Help others to answer positively too. The results will be rewarding both psychologically and financially.

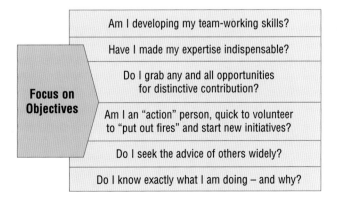

Focus on Objectives

- Am I developing my team-working skills?
- Have I made my expertise indispensable?
- Do I grab any and all opportunities for distinctive contribution?
- Am I an "action" person, quick to volunteer to "put out fires" and start new initiatives?
- Do I seek the advice of others widely?
- Do I know exactly what I am doing – and why?

TOM PETERS

3 Responding to the customer

According to Peters, "total customer responsiveness" is essential. Make it your prime objective. To achieve this, you must be flexible and ready to handle every situation. You cannot respond totally to customers by "perfecting routines" – the exceptional will inevitably occur for which a standard response will be inappropriate. Contact customers as often as you can and find out what you need to do to improve the relationship. Act on what they tell you.

Dealing with customers

Check your customer responsiveness by completing these statements:
- I last spoke to a customer ____ days ago.
- I target myself to talk to ____ customers every month.
- I reply to customers' letters within 24 hours/3 days/a week.
- I ring customers back within 24 hours/3 days/a week.
- I always/sometimes/never ask customers if they have any complaints or criticisms.
- I always/sometimes/never set targets for improving quality and meet them.
- I always/sometimes/never look out for "little things" that please customers and supply those benefits.

This should help you to understand more about responding to customers. But you can go further than this: step into the shoes of your customers to determine how they view you and your organization. Remember that most customers who have cause to complain say nothing, but may well take their business elsewhere.

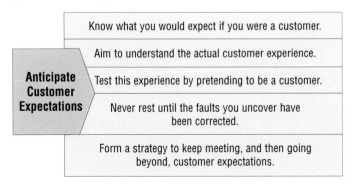

Anticipate Customer Expectations

Know what you would expect if you were a customer.

Aim to understand the actual customer experience.

Test this experience by pretending to be a customer.

Never rest until the faults you uncover have been corrected.

Form a strategy to keep meeting, and then going beyond, customer expectations.

Keeping it small

Most managers work in large organizations that, by virtue of their size, tend to be very inflexible. Whatever the size of your firm, follow the model that Peters recommends – the small one.

Subdividing into small groups

Peters reverses the long-held view that large companies have superior management practices. In "a world turned upside down" by social, economic, and technological forces, the large company needs what comes second nature to the small. That should be easier than it is, because large companies naturally subdivide into myriads of smaller groups, and even the biggest of these subdivisions will not have many people. The issue is not one of size, but whether the group can exploit the advantages of smallness.

The Advantages of Smallness
Everybody knows everybody else, which makes teamwork easier.
Action is taken faster because there is no chain of command.
Communications and sharing of information are much easier.
People identify more readily with the group and its purposes.
Everyone can share in decision-making and other so-called "management" processes.

Applying effort

None of these advantages, though, comes about by itself. They all require positive effort, and there is no reason why that effort cannot be widely applied across the organization.

- Make friends and acquaintances. This is vital, not just for use in your present organization, but also when you move on. Peters lays great stress on having a filing system of useful names, which is a vital part of your personal capital.
- Take responsibility when action is delayed or does not take place. Do not sit back and let it happen. Try to hurry things along to a positive conclusion.

- Keep talking to your colleagues, and listen to what they have to say. If you do not have the information you need, do not feel you should continue without it. Ask for it.
- Be an enthusiast for the group, its task, and its future.
- Do not be a one-man band or an isolationist. Be sure to involve others in your decisions and work, and take a close interest in what they decide and do.
- Finally... AIM BIG – BUT THINK SMALL.

Creating skunkworks

You can, to a certain extent, create the atmosphere of one of Peters' beloved skunkworks (see pp. 41 and 64–5). Skunkworks are usually set up away from the main operation and peopled by teams of creative and innovative staff who tackle a specific project from start to finish with total responsibility for its achievement.

To create an effective skunkworks that follows Peters' principles, adhere to the following guidelines:

- Recruit new staff with care. Be convinced that they will get on well with the existing members of the team and that they are experts in specific areas.
- Create heroes by giving people clear opportunities to succeed and applauding their success.
- Offer members of the team exceptional rewards that are linked mainly to the exceptional achievements of the group.
- Create a "can-do" culture based on rapid response and continuous training and development.
- Inside the skunkworks have full and genuine, informal consultations and discussions of all issues.
- Focus on a clearly defined, shared purpose.

Have great ambitions

Taking a flexible approach to your business makes it easier to achieve your ambitions. Start in a small way and build from there. Peters advises that these "small starts for small markets" should aim at practical applications. His advice applies in equal measure to small firms and large. It is a new version of the famous acronym KISS (Keep It Simple, Stupid!)... KEEP IT SMALL, STUPID!.

4

Small is very beautiful

Teaching the lessons of excellent small businesses to large companies ● **How new management theories ignore the issues of creativity and zest** ● Erasing "change" from your vocabulary and substituting "abandonment" and "revolution" ● **Why an accelerated pace of change demands crazy management for crazy times** ● The eight-point programme for generating "a whirlpool of incessant, exciting activity" ● **Learning about the "new corporate metabolism"** ● Why employees should be loyal only to their own list of contacts

Management gurus have generally sought to offer smaller companies lessons drawn from large ones. Peters has reversed this flow, learning from small companies, such as a Mid-West plumber, and offering these parables to management at large. Even in *In Search of Excellence*, Peters hymned the virtues of staying small; he and Waterman thought then that those virtues could be practised within large corporations. They maintained:

"The message from the excellent companies we reviewed was invariably the same. Small, independent new venture teams at 3M (by the hundred); small divisions at Johnson & Johnson (over 150 in a $5 billion firm); 90 PCCs at TI; the product champion-led teams at IBM; 'bootlegging teams' at GE; small, ever-changing segments at Digital; new boutiques monthly at Bloomingdale's... Small is beautiful."

That message was part of the reassurance that *Excellence* offered to large companies, who were, of course, also McKinsey's clients. They could have all the benefits of being small, while continuing to luxuriate in the strengths, prestige, and rewards of the big corporation. But new venture teams, small divisions, and "champions" could only make their contribution within the overall corporate context. The device itself accomplishes little; it's how the big company uses smallness that makes the difference, and Peters became increasingly and sharply critical of their inability to have their large cake and eat it in small slices.

Freeing management

Condemning all big companies as "crap" came much easier to a man who had left behind the large corporate world and large fees of McKinsey. The switch to smaller companies even had a virtue, since in every economy they far outnumber the large. Peters greatly widened his potential market by turning against giants in favour of pygmies – and the switch by no means removed the giants from his potential audience. When Peters offered the lessons of smaller companies not only to their owners and managers but to large corporates, the latter proved highly amenable to the idea that they could learn from plumbers. Most did not apply the lessons, of course, but that was hardly the teacher's (or preacher's) fault.

As Peters moved further and further away from the big company world, so the advice he gave and the language he used diverged more and more radically from anything a McKinsey consultant might have offered. His book *Liberation Management*, published in 1992, advises managers to "get fired", "take off your shoes", and "race yaks". The title aptly summed up Peters' feelings about the imprisoned manager. But the book did not approach the spectacular success of *Thriving on Chaos*, which was on the *New York Times* bestseller list for 60 weeks. Maybe managers did not want to be liberated.

That, at any rate, appeared to be the author's conclusion. "What has kept me awake at night since writing *Liberation Management* is the growing realization of how stale, dull, and boring most organizations are," he stated. Peters looked at the "new theories of management" and found them painfully wanting. He felt that they steadfastly ignored "the issues of creativity and zest", and actually implied strangling the former and suppressing the latter, even though the pair had become "the prime creators of economic value". Having defined the gap, Peters headed straight for it. He decided that he needed a new clarion call and a new banner.

Going beyond change

The new banner – "crazy times call for crazy organizations" – appeared beneath an oddly bland main title: *The Tom Peters Seminar*, Peters' next book, published in 1994. "Change management" had become a major theme at other gurus' seminars and inside companies. Peters noted that a "relentless refrain" preached the need to learn how to "deal with change, thrive on it" – and he shot the message down in flames: "Astoundingly, we must move beyond change and embrace nothing less than the literal abandonment of the conventions that brought us to this point. Eradicate 'change' from your vocabulary. Substitute 'abandonment' or 'revolution' instead."

This came from the man who, only half-a-dozen years before, had ordered leaders to become "obsessive about change" and to evaluate everyone on "his or her love of change". The apparent inconsistency did not bother Peters at all. It was not only change that he had left behind. His new gospel preached the need to go beyond change, and decentralization, and empowerment, and loyalty, and disintegration, and reengineering, and learning, as well as TQM (Total Quality Management, see p. 93).

Given that most organizations had not embraced many of these concepts (if any), Peters was making the most extraordinary demands. He was asking managements to leapfrog the very latest ideas in order to enter uncharted areas. His thinking was now dominated by an accelerated pace of change that made seven years seem like several lifetimes. The essence of craziness was acceleration. He noted that a laptop launched in February 1993 and bought by him in June had been discontinued by the December of the same year – and that, by the standards of the later Nineties, was a long PC life-cycle.

The crazy life-cycle

Against this background, Peters constructed a life-cycle for crazy management. First, managers had to recognize that crazy times called for more intellect and imagination. This, in turn, demanded a succession of radical developments that turned the manager into a business entrepreneur and the company into a whirlpool of incessant, exciting activity:

- "Deconstruct" the company, eliminating bureaucratic structure and sub-dividing into "spunky units".
- Make every person a businessperson.
- Develop in all employees "the mindset of an independent contractor".
- Create an organizational network ("the corporation as Rolodex").
- Leverage knowledge by "creating a corporate talk show".
- Change the bland organization into a "curious corporation".
- Go beyond looking at "Things Gone Wrong" (TGW) and "Things Gone Right" (TGR) to the creation of excitement – Wow!.
- Do it all over again, accepting the need for perpetual revolution.

Peters presented his programme as an evolution. As companies moved from stage to stage they built on the demolition work already completed as they knocked down yet another fortress of the old management. Once again, however, Peters was less radical than he appeared (or boasted). The language was often racy and gimmicky: a "gotta unit" was one of modest size which "routinely does the impossible.... Without that effort, it goes out of business. Kaput... they do it 'cause they gotta'." But much of the writing was standard business book prose, just as the argument relied for support on Peters' old standards of cases, quotes, anecdotes, and data.

The new prescriptions reflected, sometimes well ahead of their general acceptance, developments in the real world: most companies actually were being broken down into more autonomous units freed from day-to-day central control; the Japanese had long insisted that all managers be trained and deployed as business people; more and more employees were being hived off (or hiving themselves off) as independent contractors to their previous employer; networking was becoming general as corporations were forced by the pressure of technology and markets to form alliances; the needs to change radically and continuously, and to adopt "knowledge management", were becoming clichés of gurudom.

The missing ingredient that Peters injected was excitement: not only excitement, but the wholesale rejection of the status quo. He had become an avid collector of eccentricities and an advocate of their cultivation, saying to seminar participants: "Forget your detailed note-taking today. Instead take a single piece of paper and simply write on it, 'every', 'abandon' and 'everything'. That's it. Then, when you get back to work, slip the page beneath the glass on your desktop. Refer to it hourly."

Using "abandonment" (a Peter Drucker word) instead of change was only part of the self-indoctrination. Among other "crazy" questions, Peters asked readers if they routinely used "hot" words like revolution, zany, weird, freaky, nuts, apeshit, and crazy itself. They were to learn about the "new corporate metabolism (voom, varoom)" and to do that learning "on the fly, for ever". Referring to the book's epigraph, "Only the paranoid survive", a phrase taken from Andrew Grove, chief executive of microprocessor king Intel, Peters mused, "How about the Paranoid Corporation?". He found it "not a bad idea, and perhaps a good one".

Realizing the vision

But was anybody in the real world actually realizing Peters' vision? Oticon, a hearing-aid manufacturer, caught his eye. Significantly, it is Danish. Since *In Search of Excellence*, with its almost exclusive use of American models, Peters had been adding more and more foreign companies, primarily European ones, to his hero roster. Under the direction of Lars Kolind, Oticon had become a self-styled "spaghetti organization", getting rid of the entire formal apparatus (departments, managers' titles,

Coining paranoia
Andrew Grove, chief executive of the giant microprocessor organization Intel, coined the phrase "only the paranoid survive". Peters approved of it and borrowed it for his book's epigraph.

secretaries, red tape, and so on) "to create a 100 per cent project-directed entity in which employees invent the tasks that need to be done, then physically arrange themselves as they see fit to get them done".

Like Oticon, companies were advised to "self-DESTRUCT (and live anew)". Peters could not shake free from his habit of compiling exhaustive checklists. But they were now full of labels ("The Age of Pygmies?") rather than instructions. Peters saw the mood of the organization as critical. He wanted it to be, not decentralized, but "atomized" into "spirited, often pint-size, subunits with their own personalities, and headed by disrespectful chiefs". The latter would be "entrepreneurized, along with every job in the business". Peters even had a recipe for "businessing" a job, detailed as follows:

- Cross-training – training in nearly all the skills required to perform the job from start to finish
- Budgeting – responsibility for the formulation, tracking, and amendment of budgets
- Quality control – quality measurement, quality monitoring, and quality improvement processes
- Autonomy – a place of one's own within a delayered, reengineered organization, as well as the authority to make decisions, including committing substantial resources (including money) without recourse to higher-ups

"... businesses, to compete, have to be not just decentralized but deorganized. The logical limit of deorganization is the entrepreneur – the business unit of one."
The Tom Peters Seminar

- Access to expertise, from instantly available staff specialists (who in effect – "no, make that in reality" – work at the beck and call of the front line) and from outside consultants as required
- Having one's own real live customers, whether they are internal or external, who enhance the businessperson's sense of ownership
- A (limitless) travel budget

The last item embodies four key points. First, you want and need people to travel. Second, if they are empowered in large matters, how can you remove that power in small ones? Third, by removing travel controls, you remove a chunk of bureaucracy. Fourth, "trust or go bust": "if the trust is missing (genuine, unstinting respect) heaven help you, your career, your firm in the changing 90s". But there was a catch to all this atomization and independence. What would happen to loyalty, the traditional cement of the organization? Peters' solution was: forget it.

Liberating individuals

The employee should try being loyal only to his or her Rolodex, to the network of contacts, inside and outside the company. Thinking like an "independent contractor" would paradoxically "up the odds" on retaining "today's big-company job (should you wish to do so)". Note the words in brackets. As Peters' thought developed, he was becoming less interested in the organization and more obsessed with liberating the intellect, imagination, and energies of the individual. He suggested that managers should frequently ask themselves the questions that a job-seeking resumé should answer:

- What the hell do I do?
- What have I actually done?
- Who among my customers will testify to it?
- What evidence is there that my skills are state of the art?
- Who new do I know, far beyond the company's walls, who will help me deal with an ever-chiller world?
- Will my year-end resumé look different from last year's?

To Peters, it was a sad fact that the average middle manager or professional staffer was unable to answer any of these questions effectively. But the resumé routine was not meant to assist a standard vertical ascent. Rather, managers were told: "Tack. Jibe. Twist. Turn. The whole (big) idea of moving 'horizontally' is critical.... 'Careers' today involve jumping around, up sideways — and occasionally down". In a "futzed-up" marketplace, nothing sat still for "more than a few nano-seconds". Peters saw that this was not a comforting message: "The bottom line is equal parts terrifying and liberating." Coping with discomfort was all up to you — up to a point.

You needed other people, and they needed you, to complete the network. Peters described this as "the process of putting the demolished companies and the independent spirits back together". The new, reassembled organization would not be a "vertical monolith": the jobs would not be the same, year after year; and employees would not be "around for the duration". For each project, employers would collect the talents they required, in much the same way as a Hollywood producer hires the cast, crew, and production staff for a movie. Peters warmly endorsed the growing practice of "outsourcing", whose most avid users farm out to suppliers everything save their own few essential core activities.

Rolodex loyalty
*Peters uses the Rolodex as a symbol to expound his views on
employee loyalty. He advocates being loyal to one's network of
contacts, as filed in the Rolodex, rather than to the organization.*

"How many people in your unit," asked Peters, "work at
home at least one day a week?" The implication in the
question is very clear: the more the better. You are hiring,
not people's presence, but their intelligence and knowledge.
But you need to do more: "We either get used to thinking
about the subtle processes of learning and sharing
knowledge in dispersed, transient networks. Or we perish."
Peters was absolutely sure that this kind of progress was
being made towards "bringing corporations into the

post-industrial, knowledge-sharing information age". But the new theories of "knowledge management" were still hard for him to pin down – and hard for others, too.

Unanswered questions

Peters wrote that "the geniuses of leveraging knowledge are the first to admit that they still have many more questions than answers". So did he. But Peters was happy as long as he had agitated minds and got people to at least ask, "What if he's even half right?" He confessed to being unsure if he was right even to that degree. The cocksure dealer in certainties of *In Search of Excellence* was now dealing tentatively with uncertainties. "The curious corporation" was still a long way away, "in this book and in business", but what was it? He could only come up apologetically with a "not that great" list of its possible policies:

- Hire curious people.
- Hire a few genuine off-the-wall sorts.
- Weed out the dullards, nurture the nuts.
- Go for youth.
- Insist that everyone take vacations.
- Support generous sabbaticals.
- Foster new interaction patterns.
- Establish clubs, bring in outsiders, support off-beat education.
- Measure curiosity.
- Seek out odd work.
- Look in the mirror.
- Teach curiosity.
- Make it fun.
- Change places.

Just as the author says, the list is not that great. *The Tom Peters Seminar* was a work in progress, peddling ideas that were semi-formed, and perhaps could never be completed. Peters concluded that "in a crazy world stable, sensible organizations make no sense". His problem is obvious: how could a preacher of "no sense" management convince managers that his own preaching made sense?

Ideas into action

- Recognize that crazy times call for more intellect and imagination.

- Leverage and spread knowledge by participating in "a corporate talk-show".

- Develop small units with their own personalities and disrespectful chiefs.

- Seek the autonomy required for making decisions and committing substantial resources.

- Think like an independent contractor, even if you are not one.

- Look for horizontal career opportunities, not the standard vertical ascent.

- Get used to thinking about sharing knowledge in transient networks.

5

Management through provocation

Provocation as a technique for galvanizing managers into radical improvement ● **Delighting the customer, not by systems, but by spontaneous Wow!** ● Developing an emotional link between customer and product or service ● **Greater efficiency as the hard-nosed way to win customer loyalty** ● How to stand out from "the growing crowd of look-alikes" ● **Why revolution has ousted change and continuous improvement** ● Moving forward through constant action and bold embrace of failure

As his thinking about management evolved, from financially oriented rationalism to people-oriented, semi-controlled anarchy, so Peters moved from cool consultant to fiery, wildly unorthodox, evangelical preacher. He now urges managers to go for "Wow!", and encourages advanced eccentricity: "crazy" management. But behind the show-biz approach there lies a sane idea: that managers need provocation, however wild it may appear, to jerk them out of established, ineffective ways, and to galvanize their businesses.

Not only is the idea rational; it can and does work. Thus, a Maltese businessman travelled all the way to Scotland to attend a Peters seminar and was inspired by the guru's provocation to tackle the problems of his beer enterprise in a radically different way. On his return to Malta, he split the brewery into units, none larger than 100 people, each headed by a general manager who was made responsible for meeting financial targets and rewarded accordingly. Sales and profits both shot up dramatically.

This solution did not result directly from Peters' teaching, however, and by no means amounts to "crazy" management. The master's contribution was to persuade the businessman to go "outside the box", to stop trying to improve his business within the confines of the established system and philosophy. When you are told to be crazy, in other words, you stop being crazy enough to run your business in an unproductive way. That is what makes sense of a paradox posed in *The Tom Peters Seminar*: "This is the craziest chapter in the book. This is the most sober chapter in the book." Its theme could have been posed by the most buttoned-up McKinsey consultant: how to "meet customers' needs in ways that will stand out in an incredibly crowded and kinetic marketplace".

Preacher teacher
Tom Peters now bears little resemblance to the McKinsey consultant he once was. Casual dress and unorthodox teaching have replaced the sober suit and conventional theories of management.

New and different

Even German managers, who are renowned for their conservatism, needed no teaching in the next proposition: quality is not enough. "New competitors from around the globe, quality-conscious all, are joining us in flooding the market with flawless products." To stand out from the crowd, new marketing strategies are needed – not just new products. They are not enough, either. They have to be new and *different*.

Peters pointed out that researchers in 1993 gave "a grade of D or F" to half the new products they tested, including entries from great companies like Procter & Gamble. The Japanese, Peters noted, had learnt the lesson. He quoted a cosmetics boss who warned that until that time Japan had relied on its technological advances and high quality to sell its products, but that would no longer be enough. Their products must now have "spirit", too.

There is a long distance between this sober truth in *The Tom Peters Seminar* and Peters' ideas in *The Pursuit of Wow!*, the title of another book published in 1994 and based substantially on his syndicated newspaper columns. Here, Peters took to extremes the new orthodoxy about the need for customer delight and excellent service, and with justification. The customer notices exceptions, good or bad, so "exceptional" service is unorthodox, "crazy" if you like. Peters cites an Auckland restaurant that has on its walls framed letters – not of praise, but of complaint. His attention is constantly caught by such details. But, then, so is that of customers.

Peters no longer tried, as in *In Search of Excellence*, to systematize his concept, because by definition customer delight is not a matter of system, but of spontaneity. Instead of prescriptions, he offered questions, such as:

"... if employees are inundated with practical customer information rather than vague exhortations, they won't be able to keep their distance. They'll begin to 'think customer' – and, maybe, even start to dream about customers."
The Pursuit of Wow!

TOM PETERS

- Is your company's average product offering ho-hum?
- Does the very act of defining [quality] precisely dessicate the product and obscure the more important elements of quality?
- Does "have fun" apply to the experience of customers dealing with your company? Should it? Could it?
- Love. Love. Love. Use that word in business?
- Are you snuggling up – boldly, proactively, lovingly – to your customers?
- Are you spending 20 per cent of your marketing budget on acquiring information about customers?

Relationship marketing

The last question came from two other consultants, Don Peppers and Martha Rogers, who wrote a book, very influential in the mid-Nineties, advocating "relationship marketing". In *The One-to-One Future* (1995), they claimed that, thanks to new technology, even the mass marketer could "assume the role of small proprietor, doing business again with individuals". The result, as mass marketers responded with enthusiasm to the thesis, was to unleash a flood of junk mail that often only dissatisfied customers, the very opposite of Peters' intentions. He was aware that relationship marketing was not the whole answer. This lay more in getting "busy adding 'Wow' to your basic products and services".

Peters conceded that putting the product second to customers, as Peppers and Rogers proposed, "is hardly a guarantee of success". But it is a condition of success. In *In Search of Excellence*, Peters and Waterman had mentioned the customer only once in their eight attributes. Managers were urged to maintain "constant contact with customers", which in itself said nothing about the latter's treatment. Now Peters regarded this treatment as fundamental. He quoted another guru, Robert Peterson, who had found "that there is a large 'affective' component to service – from the customer's view". To win repeat business (an acid test), firms had to develop "an emotional link" between the customer and the product or service.

That message resonated for an emotional man like Peters. He made a film on the subject, which was produced by Video Arts, and called it *Service with Soul*. Built around a live seminar, the film sang the praises of new heroes who went to extraordinary, deeply committed, and caring lengths to gratify the customer. Yet, even in Peters' vehement presentation, these hero managements do not really seem "crazy", or to be operating in a crazy environment. They include, for instance, plumbers and suppliers of plastic mouldings – what might be called "ho-hum" businesses which for the most part have been barely touched by the digital revolution, the upheavals in consumer markets, and the acceleration of change.

Supplier partnerships

Peters' emphasis on the revolutionary environment and the threat of change, though, is part of the provocation process. With the plastics firm, Nypro, which had adopted a commonsense but radical strategy, Peters' purpose was to provoke others into showing similar readiness to adopt new ideas and abandon old ones. Nypro had become a prime exponent of "supplier partnership", a rapidly spreading trend in which the two sides of a business relationship cooperate on all aspects of the product or service. Vistakon, the Johnson & Johnson subsidiary that makes disposable contact lenses, links with this supplier "to assess production processes, product quality and productivity" in meetings that last for two days every six weeks. The computer links between the two enable Vistakon in Florida to check on Nypro's "real-time performance" in Massachusetts: "how many units are being produced, the amount of waste, even the on-line statistical process control numbers". For their part, Nypro managers can use the computers to get equally detailed information from Vistakon. By acting on the pooled, once-private information, the partners get extraordinary results, such as a billion moulds delivered to Vistakon without a single late shipment or quality defect, and cuts in the customer's annual costs that have run from 5 per cent to 20 per cent.

This operation would win the total approval of experts in TQM (Total Quality Management), a hard-nosed business discipline, focusing the entire organization on achieving higher quality of all products and processes, that does not work in terms of the undisciplined pursuit of "Wow!". Peters was equating the pursuit of operating efficiency with the achievement of an "intimate relationship" with the customer. In fact, the intimacy in this case was the only way to optimize the efficiency; the two attributes, like the Vistakon and Nypro technical teams, are Siamese twins. Likewise, a Californian plumbing firm called De-Mar used greater efficiency as its prime weapon in winning customer loyalty. According to the *Service with Soul* video, De-Mar's basic offering is simple:

- Standardize prices and list them.
- Provide service round the clock, seven days a week, on the day of the enquiry.
- Guarantee all work for one year.

Customer service

Peters was attracted by the methods that De-Mar's proprietor, Larry Harmon, used to achieve these aims, such as 6-a.m. training sessions (part of a sustained training programme) that start with Harmon shouting, "Can I get an amen!" at the "Service Advisers", that is, plumbers. Their pay depends on a points system that measures six aspects of customer service. Good phone calls about the Advisers, good letters, and customer requests for a named Adviser earn respectively 1,000, 2,000, and 1,000 points. Bad phone calls, bad letters, and "does not want Adviser back" rate minuses of 1,000, 2,000, and 2,000 points.

Harmon is not much good at hiring (in one year half his hires were fired), but he is plainly a highly effective manager and good at motivating his employees. The familiar doubt arises, however. Will what works for one company or one manager in one business transfer to another company, manager, or business? Peters' own answer, strangely, is "No". On the contrary, companies need, above all, to be different from one another, "standing out from the growing crowd of look-alikes". The hero companies, on this reading, can no longer act as role models to other companies. They are provocations, stimuli for "generating yeasty responses – personal and corporate – to these very yeasty and frequently frightening times".

"In the age of e-mail, supercomputer power on the desktop, the Internet, and the raucous global village, attentiveness – a token of human kindness – is the greatest gift we can give someone."
The Pursuit of Wow!

Yet the books published by Peters in 1994 belied his own thesis. If management is not a generic subject, how could Peters theorize on its conduct? If customer-supplier partnerships, as applied by the businesses Nypro and Vistakon (see pp. 92–3), achieved superior results for both parties, would not the same be true for other businesses with different products? If companies aiming, like De-Mar, to achieve excellence in customer service successfully linked reward to that excellence, why would that not work generally? Having founded his career on the creation of management templates, Peters now argued that they were impossible, while, at the same time, perversely continuing to endorse transferrable, imitable procedures.

Disorganized and disjointed

Peters gave up trying to resolve the paradox in *The Pursuit of Wow!*. This book tackles all the problems posed by a disorganized, disjointed world by being disorganized and disjointed itself. It makes almost no attempt at coherence, unlike *The Tom Peters Seminar*, which is tightly organized, each chapter leading on to the next, and the whole forming an integrated theory of management. In *The Pursuit of Wow!*, Peters lets his long experience of business "lead my mind where it will". The result is a hotch-potch of 210 homilies and quotations, brief case histories and anecdotes, management theory and maxims. It all leads up to a pained lament: "My average seminar participant comes dressed in a drab suit, uses drab language – and noticeably quivers when I suggest that the most likely path to career salvation is to get fired. Do you know how depressing it is to look out at a sea of cookie-cutter clean-cut faces?"

The lavish income Peters earned from the seminars did little to ease the pain: "Even at my obscene rates, it's discouraging," he complained. He often had "to fight an urge to... scream" at this unpromising audience: "Ye gads, wake up! Breathe! Go down swinging. Try something. Try *anything*. Be A-L-I-V-E, for heaven's sake!" The *agent provocateur* had a clientele that refused to be provoked. But you could hardly blame them. In the real world, people still

Small is beautiful
Richard Branson of the Virgin Group is seen by Peters as a "small-unit, split-'em-when-they-grow-big guy" who says that, above 50 or 60, people "get lost in the corridors of power".

want careers. Managers are still responsible for seeing that their businesses are competently and honestly administered. Schedules must still be drawn up and adhered to. Middle managers are still required for all kinds of non-crazy purposes.

How crazy, in reality, can a company become? In *The Witch Doctors*, the co-authors John Mickelthwait and Adrian Wooldridge, who both write for *The Economist*, criticize Peters' extreme "anti-rationalist stand". They disparage his approach: "The world has gone bonkers, he rants, and to cope with it we must go bonkers too." They accuse him of arguing mistakenly that managers must abandon their attempts to manage scientifically and turn themselves from careerists into entrepreneurs. They criticize the idea that cutting down on bureaucracy and hierarchy is old hat, and that companies should rather abandon any attempt at central control in order to set free the energies and initiatives of the people they employ – who can themselves be as crazy as they like – in fact, the crazier the better.

The critique is fair. But Peters, as so often, is making an extreme statement of a rational and, indeed, generally accepted thesis. In calmer tones, he himself writes: "Change and constant improvement (*kaizen* per the Japanese), the watchword of the Eighties, are no longer enough. Not even close." In going on from that observation and calling for "revolution, and perpetual revolution at that", Peters was singing much the same song as most gurus. Nor was there anything "crazy" about a statement like this: "only a bias for constant action [echoing, curiously enough, one of the eight attributes featured in *Excellence*] and a bold embrace of failure, big as well as small, will move companies forward".

Constant disequilibrium

Peters approvingly quotes "management grandee Peter Drucker", who is the arch-apostle of sanity: "The most probable assumption is that no currently working 'business theory' will be valid ten years hence." Managers, concluded Peters, had to thrive "amidst constant disequilibrium". The finishing line in the corporate race kept changing, even for companies that successfully practised "The Five Virtues". These were presented with supporting examples, quoted from specific "transformation leaders":

■ *"Pedal to the metal"* – i.e., put your foot right down on the accelerator and keep it there. ("Organizations are capable of taking on more than their leaders give them credit for")

■ *Action* ("put our heads down [and] engineer like mad")

■ *Embrace failure* ("he [Branson] doesn't give a f...")

■ *No tepid responses* ("make something great")

■ *Focus amidst mayhem* ("you've got 12 minutes")

The evocation of individual leaders, such as Richard Branson of Virgin, Ed McCracken of Silicon Graphics, and textile tycoon Roger Milliken, emphasizes the overweening importance of the dynamic boss in transformation. Even if some of the business idols develop clay feet, Peters never loses his faith in the super-star CEO, who is always, "Pushing the needle all the way over, unabashedly championing revolution, and getting the company anarchists to the barricades." This "great man" theory of management sits uncomfortably with Peters' cult of the self-managing, self-realizing individual ("reinventing civilization begins with reinventing thee and me"). But it is the unifying theory of all his thought, from *Excellence* onwards.

It is not possible to achieve extraordinary results without extraordinary people at the top, and you know they are extraordinary because of their extraordinary results. The tautology is basic to Peters' research and teaching. Like any good hot gospeller, he preaches in parables. The faith is more important than the logic, and the passion outweighs the intellect. Yet logic and intelligence do underlie Peters' thought, and they provide its enduring value. The idea that organizations can confine and suffocate the talents and ambitions of individuals is not new. But Peters the prophet is needed to provoke managers into recognizing this stupidity for what it is, and to strive to be both different and better.

Ideas into action

- Think "outside the box" to fundamentally improve the business system.

- Keep on questioning every aspect of the business, especially service.

- Found your "crazy" initiatives on solid, commonsense ways of serving customers.

- Link up with suppliers and customers to share improved efficiency.

- To achieve superior service, link rewards to measured customer satisfaction.

- Try radically new and different ideas whenever you get the chance.

- Know that your organization can do more than you expect.

Replacing rationality with anarchy

In *The Tom Peters Seminar*, Peters pronounced that "The one mistake I'm not making with this book that I've made in some (all) of the others is to think that I've arrived at THE ONE ANSWER FOR ALL TIME."

That would no doubt surprise the people who paid up to $1,000 apiece to attend the seminars from which the book was derived, for Peters exudes conviction as he expounds his doctrines. He truly believes in what he is saying, but only while he is saying it. In the early Nineties, he concluded that successful businesses had to follow much the same line: nothing is for ever, or even for long. He approvingly quoted a consultant named Roger Martin: "Whatever you've built, the best thing you can do... is to burn it down every few years.... Don't change it, but b-u-r-n i-t d-o-w-n."

In a world where the outrageous has become the norm, Peters made outrage his norm, too, appearing on the cover of *Seminar* in multi-coloured boxer shorts. He became ever more fervent in his attack on traditional forms. The doctrines he started to preach through every medium, from seminars to CD-ROMs, drummed home the theme

"Crazy Times Call for Crazy Organizations" and won him vast fees and an enthusiastic following.

Charismatic entertainer

Peters had become the nearest thing yet to a management Messiah. His seminars resembled revivalist meetings rather than management lectures. He had learnt to match his physical energy to the vehemence of his message. Marching among his audience with a microphone, backed up by dramatic visual aids, Peters harangued people, who applauded enthusiastically, but who mostly did not put his precepts, or anything like them, into practice. Peters was now a successful entertainer, but that was weakening his reputation as a serious management thinker.

Now living in Silicon Valley, he had unrivalled opportunities to observe the management of its successful firms. They practised the free-wheeling, responsive, and highly entrepreneurial style he favoured, starting small and sub-dividing all the time to avoid

"We're flattening our organizations, shedding our bureaucratic excesses. That's good – and long overdue. But as to entering the Age of Imagination, we're just barely sniffing at the doorway." *The Tom Peters Seminar*

the blight of bigness. Yet his two 1994 books made scant reference to the Valley or to its micro-electronic multi-millionaires and billionaires, such as Bill Gates.

The likes of Gates responded to change and challenge with all the speed and flexibility that Peters had been demanding. But they were not anarchists; they were highly disciplined empire-building businessmen, ruled by logic, not by WOW!.

In *Excellence*, Peters had promoted large corporate businesses, to which he remained faithful, though increasingly critical, for some years. Then he transferred his allegiance to medium and smaller enterprises, with a sprinkling of large-scale corporate heroes. But neither of these audiences came along for the whole of his revolutionary ride. His abandonment of rationality had left Peters without a constituency. To change the metaphor, the followers still came to worship, but there was no church, just a fiery preacher of easily ignored sermons.

Finding method in madness

The Peters mantra, "crazy times call for crazy organizations", sounds crazy itself. But the author is perfectly sane. Separate out the hype and exaggeration and the underlying message is one that all managers should heed: prepare to reinvent yourself and embrace change.

The new orthodoxy
According to Peters, nothing is for ever. Orthodoxy itself is changing. To succeed in management, you need to move towards the new orthodoxy − or the orthodoxy of the moment. Already managers are having to learn how to work in organizations that have moved decisively from traditional vertical structures towards horizontal ones. In these more flexible companies autonomous units, or even temporary ones, are the key building blocks.

Developing skills
The new orthodoxy requires managers with all-round business skills. You need to be as knowledgable as an independent contractor, which is what many people have become. Already, your dependence on people networks, both inside and outside the organization, is far greater than that of previous generations. Increasingly your day-to-day work, and what you ultimately produce and sell, involves more knowledge (or "software") and relatively less "hardware".

The certainty of change
This intellect-dominated output is what is required by today's market, which places a large premium on what is new. It demands that you must be intellectually inquisitive and productive. Managing efficiently is important, but it is no longer enough. The only certainty in today's environment is that it is continually changing. To meet this challenge, strive to reach ever higher levels of effectiveness and adaptability.

Revolutionary management
Peters calls this process the "perpetual revolution". To deal with this new state of affairs, aim to be an eminently sound and successful business manager as well as the revolutionary that Peters describes.

1 Meaning business

Mastering the principles of business is anything but crazy. Peters stressed that all managers must "know the business". Work to understand fully not just your own function but business generally.

Understand business

Knowing the business means knowing the economic and financial consequences of your own actions, as well as the economics of the entire company. To do this, you need the following skills.

The Essential Business Skills
Understanding and being able to write a business plan
Understanding and being able to write a budget
Distinguishing between direct and indirect costs
Distinguishing between profit and contribution
Analyzing marginal costs
Appreciating the concept of "opportunity cost"
Defining and applying standard financial measures such as return on capital, return on equity, cash flow, and gross margins
Knowing how to use Pareto's Law

The amount of information available to you is endless, but unless you have and use the basic tools listed above your business knowledge, or equipment, will be seriously deficient.

Applying knowledge

By using these skills you are better placed to put Peters' ideas into action. For instance, Pareto's Law separates the "insignificant many" from the "significant few". This is the 20/80 rule. So 20 per cent of your customers contribute 80 per cent of sales or profits. To be an effective manager, concentrate the bulk of your efforts on the significant fifth of customers and find low-cost ways of serving the rest. Ineffective managers treat all customers equally.

Adding value

The financial skills are essential tools for ensuring that you make a real profit and optimize your financial return. Take, for example, indirect costs, or overheads. The higher the overheads in relation to sales revenue, the harder it is harder to earn a profit. The ideal is to charge the best possible price but also keep a tight control on costs.

However, Peters emphasized that cost reduction is not the only priority. Some expenditure is vital, for instance on innovation, quality, and customer service. Anything that damages a customer's perception of your business will damage the business. The pursuit of excellence means striving always to enhance the value of the business.

Taking control

Managers are often told to run their section of a company like their own business. Ask yourself how you might act if the business really was your own, and you could organize it as you wished:

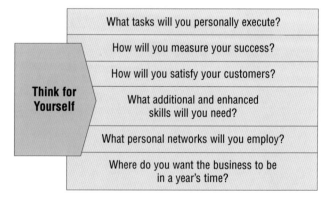

Think for Yourself	What tasks will you personally execute?
	How will you measure your success?
	How will you satisfy your customers?
	What additional and enhanced skills will you need?
	What personal networks will you employ?
	Where do you want the business to be in a year's time?

Knowledge is strength

You will certainly need to answer these questions if you do become an independent contractor – an increasingly likely option today. Keep asking the questions until the answers become instinctive. At the same time, take every opportunity to increase your knowledge – and do not stop with yourself. The "open-book" style of management allows everyone to know key numbers, results, and plans. The stronger everyone's knowledge of the business, and the more they can put that knowledge into action, the stronger the whole operation.

2 Living with change

You are living in an unsettled, dynamic world, where change is the only constant. Take a moment to write a list of your latest significant purchases and your current interests. How many of them would have been on the same list a decade ago? Five years back? Last year? Even if the purchases and interests are similar, the way you buy and pursue them will almost certainly have changed.

Think differently

These changes also affect your customers. They are constantly seeking novelty and differentiation. Peters stresses the need for new and different thinking. He urges you to develop a new mentality:

- List the products and/or services your company offers and ask "Are they scintillating? Dazzling?"
- Ensure that you and your colleagues appreciate the shift towards services and intellectual components, and adjust your priorities to reflect the importance of these "soft products".
- Be seriously imaginative.
- Subject processes and products to continuous, impersonal scrutiny, and drop those that are outdated.

Act differently

You cannot respond to changing market needs unless you are open to change yourself. Adopt new practices to meet new conditions.

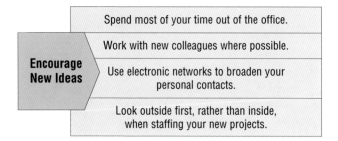

Encourage New Ideas
- Spend most of your time out of the office.
- Work with new colleagues where possible.
- Use electronic networks to broaden your personal contacts.
- Look outside first, rather than inside, when staffing your new projects.

Above all, create excitement for your colleagues and your customers. Peters tells you to ask "On a scale of 1 to 10, how dull is your unit, your company, your closest competitor? How dull are you?" Be honest with your answers – and make a commitment to banish dullness.

3 Managing your career

Whether or not you choose to stay in the corporate world, take responsibility for developing your own career – do not leave it up to your company. Peters' advice is to "think independent".

Manage yourself

Be prepared to move jobs and companies. Keep updating your curriculum vitae every six months. Follow Peters' recommendations for taking control of your own destiny:

Take Charge of Your Career	Look on training as your personal research and development spending.
	Learn to work effectively at home.
	Add useful and potentially useful names to your contact list every day.
	Accept that your first loyalty is to yourself.

As the security of a job for life fades into the past, you need to be able to survive in today's chaotic marketplace. Equip yourself as well as you can for a "non-linear, opportunistic" career.

Competence is the key

Peters poses a key question: "What do you want to be famous for?". The answer should be "Towering competence". Your obligation to yourself demands nothing less. Achieving and applying that competence also justifies your employment by others, since that is how you meet your obligation to them. Take every opportunity to develop your competence.

■ Draw up and follow a learning plan that you review every three months.

■ Design your own job (as far as you can).

■ Act on your own initiative wherever possible.

■ Learn from colleagues the secrets of their success.

Above all, keep looking for career moves, not necessarily promotions, that will teach you "something new and special", associate you with talented people, and confront you with a tough challenge.

TOM PETERS

Managing by provocation

There is a very sane reason for Peters' extrovert, show-biz approach. Shock tactics are needed to provoke action. To thrive in chaos, think and act in completely new ways.

Provoking a response

Much of Peters' teaching seems to have little to do with management and more to do with paradox. Take these maxims:

- Success begets failure.
- Fiction beats non-fiction.
- Unintended consequences outnumber intended consequences.
- Reject simple explanations.

In contrast, conventional management teaching uses hard statistics. For example, Forum Corporation's research tellingly revealed that 70 per cent of customers deserted major manufacturers not because of price or quality problems, but because they did not like "the human side" of doing business with the supplier. The aim of both approaches is to provoke you into action.

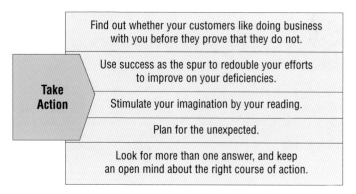

Take Action

Find out whether your customers like doing business with you before they prove that they do not.

Use success as the spur to redouble your efforts to improve on your deficiencies.

Stimulate your imagination by your reading.

Plan for the unexpected.

Look for more than one answer, and keep an open mind about the right course of action.

Searching for excellence

Provocation jerks you out of your rut and into new and more effective ways of acting. "One-minute excellence" is one of the most useful Peters provocations of all. It means deciding to act now: "You do it and it's done.... As of this second, quit doing less-than-excellent work". This is the language of the seminar guru and the showman. But why not take up the challenge?

GLOSSARY

ATHOS, ANTHONY: Expert on corporate cultures who worked on the McKinsey "exellent company project" with Peters and Waterman.

ATOMIZATION: The restructuring of an organization into small subunits headed by individual managers.

AUSTIN, NANCY: Peters' co-author of *A Passion for Excellence.*

BACK TO BASICS: The rejection of conventional and complex theories of business management in favour of key concepts such as value and vision.

CRAZY ORGANIZATIONS: Organizations that are not built around continuity and routine, but vigorously promote "creativity and zest" as the drivers of profits, growth, and economic success.

CREATIVE SWIPING: The taking of innovative ideas from sources outside the business organization.

"EXCELLENT COMPANY" PROJECT: McKinsey research project, undertaken primarily by Peters and Waterman, to discover what distinguished the companies that excelled from others.

FLEXIBILITY: Making organizations responsive to unpredictable external change by having highly adaptable structures in which managers can react with anti-bureaucratic urgency, operationally and in strategic planning.

FORTUNE 500: Annual list compiled by *Fortune* magazine giving the top 500 US companies by sales.

HORIZONTAL MANAGEMENT: Non-hierarchical structure of management.

KNOWLEDGE WORKERS: Workers who "identify themselves by their own knowledge rather than by the organizations that pay them" (Drucker).

LOOSE-TIGHT CONTROLS: In the running of a company, a mix of staff autonomy to encourage creativity and innovation, and centralized control over finance and reporting.

MBWA (MANAGEMENT BY WANDERING AROUND): Interventionist, out-of-the-office, hands-on top management.

McKINSEY & COMPANY: Management consultancy based in New York where Peters worked from 1974 to 1981.

SCALE ECONOMIES: The reduction of production costs per unit of sale as numbers of units produced increase.

SCIENTIFIC MANAGEMENT: Efficiency theory developed by Frederick Taylor in the late 19th and early 20th centuries, which formed the basis of what became known as "work study".

SEVEN-S FORMULA: McKinsey analysis of an organization, based on structure, strategy, systems, style of management, skills, staff, and shared values.

SKUNKS: The creative iconoclasts, rule-breakers, and individualists within an organization who are prepared to think freely and be innovative away from the company's bureaucracy.

SKUNKWORKS: Separate, decentralized working premises for skunks; named after the Skunkworks established by Kelly Johnson at Lockheed in Burbank, California, after the Second World War.

STICKING TO THE KNITTING: The precept that companies should stay with the business they know, concentrating on their strengths and rejecting diversification.

TOM PETERS GROUP: Peters' management training organization located in Palo Alto, Silicon Valley.

TOP-DOWN POLICIES: Policies dictated by top management.

TQM (TOTAL QUALITY MANAGEMENT): A management system that trains all employees in the techniques and application of quality improvement.

WATERMAN, ROBERT: Former McKinsey consultant and Peters' co-author of *In Search of Excellence.*

BIBLIOGRAPHY

Tom Peters had such a huge success with his first, co-written book, *In Search of Excellence*, that even the multi-million sales of his subsequent half-dozen books are dwarfed by that extraordinary hit. Written with Robert Waterman, *Excellence* is still in print, although its corporate examples and principal ideas have been left far behind, not least by Peters himself.

Peters' latest book, *The Circle of Innovation* (1999, Random House, New York), takes up one of the major themes that have run through his work since the days of *Excellence*. It is described as "a practical handbook for turning any organization into a perpetual innovation machine". Peters sees his books as management tools: the subtitle for *Chaos* was "Handbook for a Management Revolution", which hardly lived up to the billing. But there is much that is practical in the *Reinventing Work* series (1999, Random House, New York), each of which (*Projects, Brand You, Professional Service Firm*) lists 50 essential points for achieving success. There is also the *Tom Peters Business School in a Box* (1995, Alfred A. Knopf, New York), and a host of video and audio cassettes.

A book on Peters by Stuart Crainer, *The Tom Peters Phenomenon* (1998, Capstone Publishing, New York), aptly sums up Peters' progress from Corporate Man to Corporate Skunk.

WORKS CITED

Peter F. Drucker (1999) *Management Challenges for the 21st Century*, HarperCollins, New York.

Don Peppers and Martha Rogers (1995) *The One-to-One Future*, Doubleday & Co., New York.

Tom Peters (1982) *In Search of Excellence*, Harper & Row, New York.

– (1987) *Thriving on Chaos*, HarperCollins, New York.

– (1989) *A Passion for Excellence*, Random House, New York.

– (1992) *Liberation Management*, Alfred A. Knopf, New York.

– (1994) *The Tom Peters Seminar*, Random House, New York.

– (1994) *The Pursuit of Wow!*, Random House, New York.

Index

Robert Heller

Robert Heller is himself a prolific author of management books. The first, *The Naked Manager*, published in 1972, established Heller as an iconoclastic, wide-ranging guide to managerial excellence – and incompetence. Heller has drawn on the extensive knowledge of managers and management acquired as the founding editor of *Management Today*, Britain's premier business magazine, which he headed for 25 years. Books such as *The Supermanagers*, *The Decision-makers*, *The Superchiefs* and (most recently), *In Search of European Excellence* have all emphasized how to succeed by using the latest ideas on change, quality, and motivation. In 1990 Heller wrote *Culture Shock*, one of the first books to describe how information technology would revolutionize management and business. Since then, as writer, lecturer, and consultant, Heller has continued to tell managers how to "Ride the Revolution". His books for Dorling Kindersley's Essential Managers series are international bestsellers.